FINANCIAL
EVOLUTION

FINANCIAL EVOLUTION

TRANSFORM

YOUR LIFE

THROUGH THE

FIVE STAGES

OF WEALTH

ERIC J. MORIN, MBA

Published by Advantage, Charleston, South Carolina.
Member of Advantage Media Group.

ADVANTAGE is a registered trademark, and the Advantage colophon is a trademark of Advantage Media Group, Inc.

Printed in the United States of America.

10 9 8 7 6 5 4 3 2 1

ISBN: 978-1-64225-095-4
LCCN: 2020901761

Cover design by Matthew Morse.
Layout design by Wesley Strickland.

This publication is designed to provide accurate and authoritative information in regard to the subject matter covered. It is sold with the understanding that the publisher is not engaged in rendering legal, accounting, or other professional services. If legal advice or other expert assistance is required, the services of a competent professional person should be sought.

Tree Neutral

Advantage Media Group is proud to be a part of the Tree Neutral® program. Tree Neutral offsets the number of trees consumed in the production and printing of this book by taking proactive steps such as planting trees in direct proportion to the number of trees used to print books. To learn more about Tree Neutral, please visit www.treeneutral.com.

Advantage Media Group is a publisher of business, self-improvement, and professional development books and online learning. We help entrepreneurs, business leaders, and professionals share their Stories, Passion, and Knowledge to help others Learn & Grow. Do you have a manuscript or book idea that you would like us to consider for publishing? Please visit advantagefamily.com or call 1.866.775.1696.

This book is dedicated to the many amazing individuals and businesses that I have had the pleasure, honor, and opportunity to work with. Each one of you is part of this story and has contributed to the creation of this book in your own way.

Thank you for being part of my story and for giving me the opportunity to be part of yours.

It is through my relationships with each and every one of you that I have realized the only true limiting factors to a person's financial success and impact are their own beliefs in what they can accomplish.

I hope that through reading this book each person realizes that there is more opportunity to make a significant impact in this world than they could ever imagine.

CONTENTS

INTRODUCTION

WHY AREN'T YOU WEALTHY YET?

It's not because you're lazy.

And it's certainly not because you aren't trying hard enough.

The sorts of people who pick up this book are the sorts of people who dream of achieving wealth and devote themselves to that dream. If you're reading this book, it means that you take nothing for granted—that you will spare no blood, spare no sweat, spare no tears pursuing your dream.

And that's what's so maddening.

You've read all the books about earning. You've read all the books about investing. You've given all of yourself to your work. You've given all of yourself to your dream. And yet you never seem to get any closer. Wealth is always just beyond your grasp.

Why?

———

For as long as I've been curious, I've been curious about wealth. What is it? How do you get it? What do you do with it once you have it?

At a young age, I started studying up. I would scour library stacks and scour bookstores, and if I saw a book about finance, I grabbed it. Anything with "wealth" in the title.

If you've ever read broadly about an issue, you'll know that the difference between two books on the same topic can be vast, but if you put together five books on the same topic, or ten books, or twenty books, they begin speaking to each other. They begin presenting a unified front. A sort of common wisdom starts to emerge—in my case, the common wisdom of America's top financial advisors.

For a while, I put that common wisdom to the test. And it didn't get me very far.

I figured that I must be missing something. So I sat down with a calculator and checked my math. I checked the common wisdom's math too. And what I realized was that the common wisdom was wrong. It was just *wrong*. The numbers didn't add up. The path that all those books had laid out for me wouldn't lead to wealth. It simply couldn't.

So I abandoned that path and began creating my own. Through trial and error, I developed an approach that would bring me success. I started creating wealth.

And that made me wonder: these financial advisors were wealthy, too, weren't they? They must have figured out the same thing that I'd figured out. So why hadn't they written about it?

> It was almost like the people who had created wealth didn't want to tell anybody else how they'd done it. And that just seemed wrong to me.

I knew myself well enough to know that I wasn't some kind of math savant. If I could figure out that the common wisdom was wrong, so could all those financial advisors who were promoting it. That meant that financial advisors' strategies were wrong, they *knew* their strategies were wrong, and they kept promoting those strategies anyway.

When financial advisors promised that their tactics would generate wealth, what they meant was that their tactics would generate wealth for *themselves*—not for their clients. Not for you. Not for me. It was almost like the people who had created wealth didn't want to tell anybody else how they'd done it. And that just seemed wrong to me.

So I started a firm devoted to helping people achieve what I'd achieved. And I discovered that even more than I enjoyed getting out of bed to generate wealth, I enjoyed getting out of bed to help *others* generate wealth—to make an impact. Sure, a part of me worried that doing this kind of work would mean putting my own wealth generation on hold. But as it turns out, if you're good at helping people, you can get paid really well to do it.

A decade later, my firm has worked with hundreds of business owners, medical and dental practice owners, consultants, and professionals, helping them to better understand wealth and the strategies they can use to attain it.

While commission-obsessed financial managers will walk right past the bullpen to get to the corner office, it's our mission to work with the entire team: the owners, the executives, the managers, and the assistants alike. Because everyone deserves access to wealth. And, contrary to common belief, professional titles have no bearing on your potential to achieve wealth. The bars to entry are the same for all of us. And the potential for success is the same too.

———

You would think that business owners would have an easier time building wealth than their team members, but the reality is that there's no difference. All of us are running in the same rat race. All of us share the mindset that if we just work harder, if we just put in more hours, if we just keep grinding, we will eventually earn enough income to generate wealth.

And all of us are wrong.

Without clear strategies and clear targets, that approach will never work.

You may be familiar with Parkinson's Law, which says that work expands to fill the time available for its completion.[1] Well, the same goes for money: our expenses generally rise to the level of our revenues. We spend what we earn. And as a consequence, we never have the opportunity to accumulate and grow wealth. That's true on the individual level and on the enterprise level.

For the sake of simplicity, let's say that to you, wealth means saving up a million dollars.

When we're given raises at work, most of us look at those raises and see spending opportunities: opportunities to buy that car, to buy that house, to upgrade our lifestyles. So we never save enough to hit that million-dollar mark. And even when we do spend carefully, on average, it takes the most diligent savers *twenty years* to put away a million dollars.[2, 3]

For most of us, that means that if we ever do make a million dollars, we won't be seeing that money until retirement. And, as it turns out, a million-dollar retirement fund isn't all it's cracked up to be. If we assume a 5 percent investment return, we're only going to be yielding $4,000 a month before taxes. And more than a quarter

---

1   The Royal Commission on the Civil Service, "Parkinson's Law," *The Economist*, https://www.economist.com/news/1955/11/19/parkinsons-law.

2   "How Long to Be a Millionaire," *The Economist*, February 11, 2013, https://www. economist.com/graphic-detail/2013/02/11/how-long-to-be-a-millionaire.

3   Analysis of previous note: "How Long Will the Average Person Take to Earn $1 Million Around the World?" *Financial Samurai*, https://www.financialsamurai.com/ how-long-will-the-average-person-take-to-earn-one-million-dollars-around-the-world.

of that monthly stipend will be eaten up by our mortgages and other housing costs.[4] So, really, we're looking at about $2,500 a month.

Not exactly lavish.

This is what I'm talking about when I say that the numbers just don't add up. Hard work and frugality won't necessarily get you a million dollars. And, even if they did, a million dollars still wouldn't make you wealthy. Once you get there, you realize that you still have a long way to go.

The same is true at the enterprise level. As business and practice owners, we tell ourselves that growth is the key to wealth: if only the business were bigger, I could generate the income that I need to be wealthy.

But just as individuals use their raises to improve their lifestyles, business and practice owners use their profits to improve their companies. As soon as money comes in, the first thing that a business owner does is reinvest that capital. We reinvest to grow. And when we grow, we reinvest again.

The upshot is that there's never any cash. It's always being used for something else.

Our intentions are good: we aren't spending recklessly, we aren't living large—we're investing responsibly. But at the end of the day, while our businesses may grow, *we* won't. We never tend to generate true wealth.

For both the individual and the owner, the expenses are always rising to meet the revenues. So we never make any progress, and we

---

4   "Median Monthly Housing Costs for Owner-Occupied Housing Units with a Mortgage," *United States Census Bureau*, 2013-2017, https://factfinder.census.gov/bkmk/table/1.0/en/ACS/17_5YR/GCT2511.US01PR.
For table parameters, see "Median Selected Monthly Owner Costs - Housing units with a mortgage and without a mortgage," Ibid, https://www.census.gov/quickfacts/fact/note/US/HSG651217.

keep repeating our daily rituals at ever-ascending levels of intensity. We get up, we get dressed, we commute, we work, we commute, we sleep, and we do it all again. We work harder. We put in more hours. We grind, and we grind, and we grind, and yet we never achieve true wealth.

The problem is that it's never enough. We set benchmarks for ourselves—goalposts that we define as wealth—and then we get there and we realize that we still aren't wealthy. So we move the goalposts. Again and again and again.

You can't build an effective strategy that way. The target is always moving. If the target's always moving, you can never hit it. And if you can never hit it, then is it really a target at all?

You need to figure out a fixed definition of wealth, or you'll never be wealthy.

━━━━

Our lives are so short—our time so precious. It's crucial that we focus on the things that matter. That's why we chase wealth: because we know that wealth will help us make the most of our lives.

But for most of us, the chase isn't going well. We know more now than we've ever known before. We're working harder now than we've ever worked before. And yet, we're still no closer to wealth. We're spinning wheels. Losing time.

So we come back to the question that got us here: Why aren't we wealthy?

It's not because we're lazy.

And it's certainly not because we aren't trying hard enough.

It's because our definition of wealth is always changing. Which is to say that we don't know what wealth is. And you can't really chase a thing—you certainly can't *catch* a thing—if you don't know what it is.

You can't possibly achieve wealth until you understand what it is. And as soon as you understand what it is, the path for pursuing it becomes clear.

> As our notions of wealth evolve, so do our strategies for pursuing it.

As this book will demonstrate over and over again, philosophy matters. The way we understand the world dictates the way that we interact with it. As our notions of wealth evolve, so do our strategies for pursuing it.

That's why it's so important to ask: What is wealth? Why do we want it? How can we get it? And what are we supposed to do with it once we have it? Those are the questions that this book will investigate.

Answering those questions will certainly involve a philosophical exploration of what we mean by "wealth." And it will also involve a practical exploration of the immediate actions that you can take to improve your fortunes. As we've seen, the two are fundamentally bound to one another: if your theories change, your practices must change too.

Over the course of the next five chapters, we will see that people pass through five discrete stages in their pursuits of wealth. At each stage, their understandings of wealth evolve, and their financial management strategies evolve too. We'll see how people transform from Dreamers to Settlers to Risk Takes to Managers to Humanitarians. We'll see the philosophies that get them there, and the strategies that follow. We'll discover which strategies are weakest, and why they fail; which strategies are strongest, and why they succeed. And, in the end, we'll discover not only the key to wealth, but also the key to a life well lived.

Because rolling out of bed without a clear mission, without a clear sense of purpose, without a defined target—doing that every day, doing that every year—makes for a shitty existence. But when you wake up with a mission—when you know what you're doing and why you're doing it—you get to start enjoying the best of what life has to offer.

———

I've been in this business for nearly two decades, and in that time, I've worked with hundreds and hundreds of people. Those collaborations—the ones that failed and the ones that flourished—have taught me that people generally show up in the world with one of three attitudes.

The first attitude says, *Poor Me.* These people have got something from their past that's still nagging at them. It won't let them go. Or, more correctly, *they* won't let go of *it*. Maybe it's the divorce they had way back in 2002. Maybe it's a market loss they suffered in 2008. Or a late-nineties real estate deal gone bad. And maybe it isn't ancient history. Maybe it's the debt they got into five years ago or the job they let go of five months ago. It doesn't matter. Because if they can't shake the past then it'll shake them—it'll shake them down for all their worth and nobody will be able to help them. Not me, not their spouses, not their kids, and certainly not their money managers. So that's the *Poor Me* approach to life.

The second attitude says, *Leave Me.* As in "leave me be." These guys think they know it all—that they've got it all figured out. And what they don't have figured out, they think nobody else can teach them. Sometimes they're lazy, but usually they're just suspicious or self-satisfied—they either can't believe or they can't stand the possibility that someone out there knows more than they do. They're so scared of being sold something that they won't listen to anyone. You could point to the sand they're standing on and tell them that there's a million dollars buried in the ground, just inches beneath their feet—that the money's theirs just so long as they'll dig for it. And these people will cross their arms, smirk, and say, "No way am I going to waste time digging. Do you have any idea what my hourly is?" They say *Leave Me*, and I say fine. You're on your own.

And then there's the third attitude—the one that says, *Transform Me*. These are the dreamers—the people who aren't wrapped up in the past, but instead are wrapped up in the future. They've got some kind of a vision—maybe not a clear vision, but a vision nonetheless—and they're willing to do whatever it takes to turn that vision into a reality.

They're never satisfied unless they're learning, unless they're growing. They're always reading, going to seminars, and challenging their most deeply held beliefs. Because, for these people, life is about building and becoming.

They know what they want to build. They know what they want to become. But they don't know how to do it. They don't know where to start. If someone would just point them in the right direction, they'd be willing to run for days without stopping.

I've devoted my career to working with these transformative people. I built my company for them. I wrote this book for them. And I hope that you're one of them. Because if you are, then you've come to the right place.

This book's for you.

STAGE ONE

1

THE
DREAMERS

LIFE IS SHORT, and we'd rather spend it enjoying wealth than spend it pursuing wealth. That's why so many of us have this ambition to acquire wealth as quickly as we can.

For me, for my clients, and I hope for you, that ambition comes with extraordinary faith: the belief that anything's possible if we try hard enough.

This first stage of the journey toward wealth is populated by *Dreamers*—people who reach for the stars, who swing for the fences, who will do whatever it takes to achieve their goals.

That commitment to our dreams and that faith in our possibilities is crucial for success. We have to carry that with us for our entire journeys, or we're lost. We have to hold onto our visions for what *could* be: the toys we want to buy, the trips we want to take, the businesses we want to create, the lives we want to lead, the legacies we want to leave behind. Without those dreams, why pursue wealth at all?

Dreamers are the best of us. They have the boldest visions and the biggest potential. And most important of all, they have *focus*. Unparalleled, unrivaled *focus*.

That focus is remarkable, admirable, enviable, crucial—but it's also more than a little bit dangerous. Because focusing on the wrong strategies can get us into big trouble. And, unfortunately, focusing on the wrong strategies is a cornerstone of this first stage on our journey toward wealth.

As far as the Dreamer is concerned, the fastest way to generate wealth is to *earn more*. The individual fights for a raise, the business owner for a better quarter. The Dreamer says that if only they had a better salary, if only they had higher revenues, if only they had *more cash*, then they would be wealthy. The dreamer figures that all they have to do to increase their wealth is increase their income.

Over the course of this book, we're going to see again and again that philosophy and practice are tied together: what you believe determines how you behave. So if you believe that income is the key to wealth, then you're going to put all of your attention on what's coming in. And you're going to put exactly none of your attention on what's going out. Namely, you'll be so focused on your earning that you'll neglect to care for your spending. And that goes both for individuals and business owners.

For the individual, the thinking usually goes that if I could just get a raise, just earn a little bit more—just inch up from $50,000 a year to $70,000 a year—then everything would change. But it won't—at least it hasn't for the hundreds of Dreamers with whom I've worked. In my experience, when your income goes up, your spending goes up to match.

That's not because Dreamers are irresponsible with their money. It's just because they're focused on their earnings and not on their savings. When new money comes in from raises and bonuses, Dreamers take those income bumps as opportunities to address big-ticket expenses that they've been putting off: they buy a car, they buy a home, and suddenly all of that new income has vanished.

And we see the same thing play out at the enterprise level all the time. For the entrepreneurial business owner and the dental/medical practice owner, the motto goes, "If I could just get revenues up, then I could finally start accumulating wealth."

How will they drive up revenues? Well, they'll invest more in marketing, invest more in team, invest more in product development. All terrific strategies for growth. And all incredibly expensive.

Every dollar you have, you spend on enterprise growth. And it works. Your business grows. But you look at your bank account, and there's nothing there. Because you've just spent it all.

So you figure that the problem is that revenues still aren't high enough. You've got to grow the company more. So every dollar that comes, you spend on enterprise growth. And it works. Your business grows. But you look at your bank account, and there's still nothing there. Because you've just spent it all. Again.

It's a vicious cycle that never generates any actual ROI. You never have any cash. That means that you never get to develop any kind of savings. And that means that when rainy days come, there's no emergency fund to dip into. Which means debt. Lots and lots of overwhelming debt.

Such is the unfair, unfortunate fate of the Dreamer. You give all of your time to your work. You neglect your family for your work. You neglect your marriage for your work. You neglect yourself for your work. And all you have to show for it is debt.

> **As long as your attention is on driving up income, you'll never be able to get any wealthier.**

Why? Because you're focused on earnings.

Both for the individual and for the owner, as long as your attention is on driving up income, you'll never be able to get any wealthier. You'll be stuck in survival mode forever, never building toward a legacy, never creating any kind of impact, and never getting to enjoy the fruits of your labor.

To get ahead, you need to start by changing your focus. You need to start by asking the right question.

ASKING THE RIGHT QUESTION

When bedtime comes around at the Morin house, we don't read our kids Dr. Seuss books. We read our kids books about wealth and personal development. And, believe it or not, they love it. Just a few nights ago, my six-year-old daughter raised her hand and asked, "Daddy, what's a capital investment?"

Children don't lack capacity; they lack teachers. Financial philosopher Jim Rohn said that.

Anyway, I once asked my eleven-year-old son whether he believed that you could get wealthy by playing the lottery. I was trying to teach him a lesson about gambling. But you can't teach kids anything. They're just too damn smart.

"It depends," he said.

"On what?" I asked.

"It depends on what you do with the winnings."

Then he went back to his YouTube show.

My son had driven right past my gambling lesson to make a larger point: that income is irrelevant. Win the lottery, don't win the lottery, it doesn't matter. What matters is what you do with the money that you're left with. Whether that's your total savings plus a million-dollar jackpot or your total savings minus the cost of a lotto ticket. Also, the key to creating wealth is the knowledge you gain along the way to create wealth. When you just win the lotto, *you did not "become more" and therefore do not know how to manage it.*

The question isn't *What do you earn?* It's *How do you manage what you earn?*

So says my son, and so say I.

I've seen this play out at work time and time again. I'm always meeting people who've won the salary jackpot, but haven't managed to generate an ounce of wealth. They're too focused on earning—never focused on managing.

Recently, a potential new client got in touch with me—a Connecticut-based executive who wanted my help generating wealth. Before we met, I asked him what had prompted him to reach out. All he said was, "Cash flow problems."

So he flew down to Atlanta to meet with me. We chatted a bit, learned a little about each other. And then I started doing some top-level data gathering.

"About how much would you say you spend per month?" I ask him.

"Oh, just a second," he says. "I've got some notes here." He pulls out his phone and swipes around for a moment. Then he says, "Okay. I've got it. What was the question?

"How much do you spend per month?" I ask again.

He has to squint over his glasses to read the screen. "$197,000," he says.

"No, no. Per *month*," I say.

He squints at the phone again, then nods. "Yep. $197,000 a month. Give or take."

For all intents and purposes, this guy has won the jackpot. In fact, if you do the math, he's got to be winning the jackpot three or four or five times a year in order to sustain that kind of spending. But, like my eleven-year-old son says, it all comes down to what you do with the winnings. This guy has virtually nothing in the bank because he doesn't know how to manage his money.

I first encountered this problem when I was about twenty-six or twenty-seven. I was working in the mortgage industry, operating out of a high-end country club. From my little office, I'd watch the club members golf out on the green, and I'd dream about someday earning what they earned.

The members at this country club and the people who came into my office seemed like they were impossibly wealthy. Fancy cars, fancy clothes, coming in to buy fancy homes. I'd look at them and wonder why they'd need a mortgage at all. I figured they could probably buy new houses with their pocket change.

And then I'd look at their bank statements. And I'd see nothing. Just *nothing*. Sure, money was coming in. Lots and lots of it. But lots and lots was going out too. And the upshot was that these people didn't have five bucks between them. Not that that mattered of course. These were the days of 100 percent financing, so they'd put zero dollars down and pocket the keys to their new megamansions—complete with pools, tennis courts, indoor theaters, the whole deal.

How they paid for groceries, I'll never know.

There was just one exception—a couple that I'll never forget.

Well, I do often forget their age: I *know* that they were in their sixties, but in my mind's eye, they're always twentysomething newlyweds. Because, unlike most of the couples I worked with, this couple seemed like they were actually *happy*. They were all over each other, kissing and smacking each other's butts.

I figured that made some kind of sense: I'd be glowing and frolicking, too, if I were about to be handed the keys to a megamansion that I couldn't afford.

But then I looked at their bank statements, and I realized I was wrong. They *could* afford their new home. In fact, they could afford to buy this new home, burn it to the ground, rebuild it, burn it to the ground, and rebuild it all over again. They had put $32 million in the bank—and those were just their *liquid* assets.

By this time, I'd already become accustomed to the idea that most big earners were going broke, so I figured that if this couple had actual wealth stowed away, their earnings must have been bigger than big. They must have been golden parachute, 1-percent-of-the-1-percent type earners.

So I pulled up their W-2s to confirm.

Turns out they weren't mega-earners. They weren't big earners. They weren't even middling earners. In their entire lives, neither of them had ever earned more than $32,000 a year. In fact, both of them were about to get new jobs. He was going to bag groceries and the wife wanted to work at an ice cream shop just for fun.

These were people who had spent their lives asking the right question—not *What do we earn?* but *How should we spend it?*—and just by asking the right question, they had begun to build themselves a fortune.

HOW SHOULD WE SPEND IT?

So that's that then. From now on, you're not going to worry about what you earn. All you're going to worry about is how you spend it. Great.

But how *should* you spend it? What's the secret to managing money for wealth? When my clients ask me that, I tell them my secret: 70/30. Spend 70 percent, save 30 percent. That's where the road to wealth begins.

SPEND 70 PERCENT ON YOUR LIFESTYLE

Whether you earn two thousand dollars a month or two *hundred* thousand dollars a month, the math is the same. Seventy percent of that income is yours to play with. And you should play unapologetically.

If you want to spend that money on a Birkin bag or Gucci loafers or a luxury vacation in Bora Bora, I don't care. Have fun. Blow it all. Live your life the way you want to live it. Just don't spend more than that 70 percent. Because 30 percent of your income is going to go toward strategic savings and investments.

That 30 percent for savings is going to get broken up into three discrete chunks of 10 percent: 10 percent for wealth accumulation, 10 percent for investment capital, and 10 percent for personal development.

SAVE 10 PERCENT FOR WEALTH ACCUMULATION

The first 10 percent of your monthly income will go toward wealth accumulation. This is your nest egg—the money that you're stockpiling with the intention of never touching it—not until retirement.

Now, if you're diligent about putting aside 10 percent every month, that nest egg's going to get real big real fast. And it's going to become tempting to start using it. No matter how much willpower you think you have, when the car breaks down, or the house gets mold, or the medical bills show up in the mail, you're going to want to spend this money. It's going to become easier and easier to justify dipping into the accumulation cookie jar.

That's why I insist that my clients put this money somewhere out of reach—brokerage accounts, retirement accounts, CDs, and so on. Those assets can stay liquid, but it's crucial that they be pulled out of your hands. Otherwise you'll start to create reasons why you need the money and need it *now*.

SAVE 10 PERCENT FOR CAPITAL INVESTMENTS

Having set aside 10 percent of your monthly income for wealth accumulation, you'll want to set aside another 10 percent for future capital investments for example an investment piece of property or a business.

Most of us know that we will someday want to purchase capital investments. But those purchases are rarely planned. We don't seek them out. We don't hunt them down. Usually what happens is that these investment opportunities sneak up on us—they surprise us. And if we aren't prepared—if we don't have money set aside—we'll miss these opportunities.

Often, these opportunities pop up during abrupt, unforeseen economic downturns. As the first law of investing says, you've got to buy low and sell high. So what better time to buy low than during a recession?

> What better time to buy low than during a recession?

We didn't know that the market was going to tank in 2008. But when it did, it offered smart savers the best purchasing environment they'd seen in decades. There's a house that I drive by every day, valued at $2.5 million. Back in 2010, after the housing bubble burst, it sold for $300,000.

That's great if you're a buyer. But you can't just be a buyer. You also have to be a saver. Because you can't buy a $2.5 million house for $300,000 if you don't have $300,000 to play with.

That's why we reserve 10 percent for future capital investments. By sticking 10 percent of your income under your mattress every month, you guarantee that you'll have cash on hand when these big opportunities come knocking.

My tween son knows this better than anyone. A year or two ago, he told me that he wanted to become an engineer. But he had a concern: "Doesn't it cost money to become an engineer and start your own firm?" he asked me. Of course, the answer was yes.

So we started a capital investment savings account for him. Every time he gets money from us, he breaks it up—giving us 30 percent to save, and keeping 70 percent to spend. And of that 30 percent, we set 10 percent aside for capital investments.

He's got a ways to go before he'll be able to finance his own engineering firm, but if in a year or two, he got the idea of starting a lemonade stand, he'd have capital investment cash ready to go.

So let me ask: If my eleven-year-old son is saving to fund his future business, don't you think you ought to start doing the same?

SAVE 10 PERCENT FOR PERSONAL DEVELOPMENT

We said that we were going to set aside 30 percent of our monthly income for savings. 10 percent of those savings went toward wealth accumulation. And 10 percent went toward capital investments. That leaves us with one last pile of 10 percent. And, as far as I'm concerned, this is the most important 10 percent of all.

It goes toward personal development.

When it comes to the personalities in personal development, a lot of people think of Tony Robbins as the ultimate guru. But some of his best stuff isn't his—he got it from Jim Rohn. And, to his credit, Tony's very candid about this.[5]

---

5   Robbins, Tony. *MONEY: Master the Game.* New York: Simon & Schuster, 2014, Chapter 3.4.

Anyway, to me, Jim Rohn is the king—the guru's guru. And the line of his that's always stuck with me is this: "In order to *have* more, you need to *become* more."[6] You need to invest in yourself.

You see, most people just *don't*. They don't invest in themselves. They can't. Because they don't set aside money for personal development. I see this all the time—new clients who will invest in a twelve-pack, but won't invest in a book. They'll invest in nightclub bottle service or $300 theater tickets, but they won't invest in a seminar.

And they're not always spending frivolously. I find that prospective clients love to invest in stocks. They'll invest in whole life insurance. In real estate. But they won't invest in themselves.

And, when I talk about investing in yourself, I don't just mean investing in *you*. I mean investing in your *life*—your friendships, your family, your marriage, your own self-education. I've had hundreds of clients with all kinds of outlandish expenses—mansions and yachts and antique sports cars—and I can tell you: there's nothing so expensive as a divorce.

If you ever want to get anywhere in this life—if you ever want to build any kind of wealth—you have to, have to, *have to* invest in your life and self-education.

And it's helpful to use that word—*invest*. I'm sure you know that one of the most important principles of investing is *compounding*. When you invest in stocks, if you double your money, the last thing you want to do is cash out. Instead, you want to put that newly earned capital back into stocks so that you can see your original investment grow exponentially. What you're doing is compounding: your money is earning money, and that money is earning you more money.

---

6   Rohn, Jim, "You Can Have More–If You Become More," *Success Presents Jim Rohn*, January 7, 2018. https://www.jimrohn.com/become-more.

Well, the investments that you make in your life work the same way. They compound. And if you don't invest in your life … well, that compounds too.

I had a client come in—the owner of a medical practice—whose personal life and business life were both in tatters. He had gotten himself stuck on the wrong side of the compound effect. You see, he hadn't been investing in himself or in his marriage. And, as a result, that marriage was falling apart. He was in the midst of a brutal divorce.

Now, those divorce proceedings were creating a lot of frustration for him, and he was taking that frustration out on his team. So the best people on his team had started quitting. As he started losing his best teammates, he started losing patients and referrals too. As referrals went down, the practice's cash flow went down. As the practice's cash flow went down, the doctor became even more stressed, and he took that stress out on the team. So even more team members quit. So referrals went down. So cash flow went down. And stress levels kept climbing.

he was caught in a vicious cycle—the compound effect gone bad.

But together, we turned revenues around. After just a few meetings with me, his practice had its biggest month *ever*.

You want to know how I got him there?

I gave him a book.

"Here's what I'm going to do," I said. "I'm going to give you a book. You have a week to read this book. And if you don't read this book, we're not going to work together."

It was a bit of a gamble. I knew that he might dislike the ultimatum. I knew that I might lose the client. But I also knew that it was the only way to help him.

A few days later, I'm in my car, and I get a call. I see that it's him. Moment of truth.

"How's the book?" I asked him.

He took a deep breath. A really deep breath. Was he about to fire me?

Nope. Turned out he just needed all that air to get him through a five-minute rave review. He didn't just like the book. He *loved* it.

So you know what I did the second week that I worked with him? I gave him another book. And another one for the third week, and another for the fourth week.

You see, he didn't need to invest more in the business. He *could*— he could have put in more money, raised salaries, bought new products, and it might have worked in the short term. But it all would have fallen apart shortly thereafter. Because the business wasn't the problem. He didn't need to invest more in the business. He needed to invest more in himself.

The more he invested in himself, the more he became excited about the world around him—his work, his team, his business, his future. He started going to work with a new kind of energy—an infectious energy. When his team asked him what the heck he was so happy about, all he'd say is, "Have you read this book? No? How about this one? Or this one? Or this one?"

Soon, his team was reading together, growing together, and, for the first time in a long time, really and truly *working* together. And that's it. That's how we turned his practice around. That's how we grew his revenues.

That doctor is living proof that if you invest just 10 percent of your income in personal development, it can radically transform your company. And personal development isn't just for business owners either. It's just as important at the individual level.

There's a misconception that individuals get paid for time spent— that if you want to earn more, what you need to do is increase the amount of time that you're working. I think that's probably because so many of us calculate our rates in terms of hours. But the reality is that you don't actually get paid for time. You get paid for value. And the way I know that is that nobody will ever pay you just to show up.

Remember Jim Rohn's classic line? It wasn't, "In order to have more, you need to *work* more." It was, "In order to have more, you need to *become* more."

If you want to earn more, you need to become the sort of person who offers more value. So that a business owner or manager says, "We couldn't live without you." When you offer that kind of value, your pay goes up. A lot. Because the business literally can't afford to lose you.

I married a dentist, and many years ago, we ran a practice together. At one point, we hired a lady for $9 an hour. And that felt fine. Until she got to know all of the patients. I mean, *she memorized their charts.* All of them. We couldn't function without her.

At a certain point, we realized that if she left, it would cost us a fortune. The quality of our service would drop, we'd lose patients, and we'd probably have to pay an arm and a leg to hire someone else who would be half as good. So we raised her salary. And then we raised it again. And again. Partly because we didn't want her to get poached, and partly because it just felt wrong not to pay her more. She was so valuable. She deserved to see that value reflected in her pay.

And so do you. If you want to start earning more, this is how you do it. You build yourself to build your wealth. Wish you had more money to devote to your lifestyle? Invest in yourself and that *70 percent's going to get a heck of a lot bigger.* Wish you had more money for capital investments? Invest in yourself. Wish you had more money to accumulate and build your wealth? Invest in yourself.

Give just 10 percent of your income to personal development, and watch all of your numbers go up.

Jim Rohn put it best. "If you work hard on your job, you can make a living," he said. "But if you work hard on yourself, you can make a fortune."[7]

SPENDER BEWARE

So the 70/30 principle says that you should put 30 percent of your monthly income into savings.

It says that 10 percent of those savings will be for *passive* accumulation. These are stacks of bills that you stick into CDs or stocks or bonds, letting them grow without much management or interference on your part.

Ten percent of those savings will be for *active* capital investments. This is money for you to go around and use, putting it to work by buying real estate or investing in a business.

And 10 percent of those savings will be for *personal development*: books, seminars, workshops, and so on.

That leaves 70 percent of your income for discretionary spending. This is your "lifestyle" money, and you should spend it without remorse. But that doesn't mean you should spend it without forethought. That's a mistake that a lot of first time savers make, and it's one that I'm hoping you'll avoid.

---

7   Rohn, Jim. "Jim Rohn on Working Harder on Yourself Than Your Job." *Success Talks*, podcast audio, August 24, 2017, https://www.success.com/jim-rohn-on-working-harder-on-yourself-than-your-job/ and https://podcasts.apple.com/us/podcast/jim-rohn-on-working-harder-on-yourself-than-your-job/id1159749342?i=1000391414105.

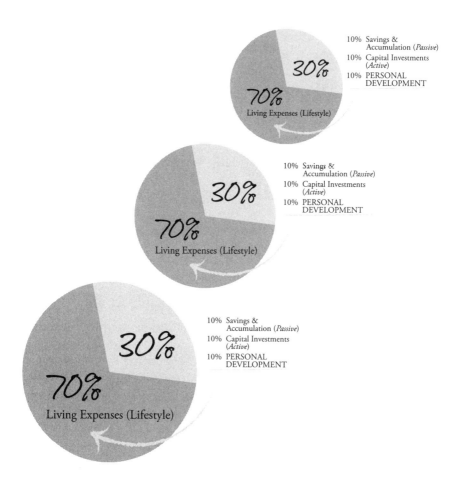

It's important to remember that lifestyle expenses aren't just big boats and beach vacations. Lifestyle expenses include the home you live in, the car you drive, the clothes you wear, the food you eat, and so on. Once you start factoring in those expenses, you start to appreciate that you can't afford to blow all of your lifestyle money in one place. A lot of that lifestyle money is already committed.

This comes up all the time in little ways. Your spouse asks whether you want to go out for dinner, and you look at your bank account, and you see that you've got $7,000 in the account. So you figure, sure, why not. But there's a very good reason why not: you don't actually have $7,000 to spend. A fair bit of that money has already been committed to other expenses.

One of those expenses is what you might call "overage." The main principle behind overage is that *stuff breaks*. The AC goes out, the car breaks down, the kids grow out of their clothes. And when stuff breaks, you've got to pay to fix it.

When you buy an AC, buy a car, decide to raise kids—those are all lifestyle choices. They might feel

You can't afford to blow all of your lifestyle money in one place. A lot of that lifestyle money is already committed.

like basic or even *necessary* lifestyle choice, but they're lifestyle choices nonetheless. They're commitments. And those commitments come with certain expenses. Some are short term—the cost to install the AC, the cost to put money down on a car, and the cost to pay for an OB. And some costs are long term—the overage costs. You don't always know what they're going to be, but you can be sure they're going to come.

In addition to overage, there are all sorts of other lifestyle expenses that a thoughtful planner can predict. The winter holidays are a good example. You know that you're going to be buying a whole lot of gifts come December. So where's that money going to come from?

Years ago, banks actually offered Christmas savings accounts. If you opted in, then every time that you made a deposit into your main checking account, the bank would take a small percentage of that money and put it in your Christmas savings account. That way, when the holidays rolled around and it came time for gift-giving, you wouldn't be caught in the lurch.

That was until banks realized that they can make a heck of a lot more money off of you when you're caught in the lurch. Now, banks *love* the lurch. You see, most people don't plan well. They don't set aside money for the holidays. So when gift-giving season comes around, they have to put their gift purchases on credit cards. Banks charge extortionist interest rates on those expenditures and wring the money out of you for weeks, months, or years to come.

These days, the banks are counting on you not to plan ahead. They know that even when we set aside 30 percent of our incomes for savings, most of us aren't accounting for little things like the holidays.

We're also usually not thinking about our regularly scheduled utility bills. And we're certainly not thinking about big-ticket items that we're going to have to replace a few months or years down the road.

Think about it: if you buy a car, you're not just committing to making payments on that one car. You're deciding that owning a car is a fundamental part of your lifestyle. Which means that you're effectively committing to buying *another* car when this one becomes too old to drive.

Sure, we've set aside 70 percent of our income for lifestyle expenses, but it's crucial that we remember: a decent portion of that money has already been committed. It's been committed to Christmas, and cars, and computers, and kids' clothes, and so on.

Once my family started accounting for those commitments, it changed the way we spent our money. Earlier in our marriage, we had joint accounts—a joint checking account, a joint debit card, joint credit cards. We always thought that we were spending reasonably. But then we'd get the monthly bill, we'd look at the total, and our jaws would drop. Twenty bucks here, fifteen bucks there—it had added up.

We decided that we wanted to be more careful about our spending, and that meant opening individual accounts. Now each of us has our own checking accounts, our own debit cards, and our own credit cards. The money in her account is hers, and the money in my accounts is mine. And that's had a tremendous effect on the way we spend.

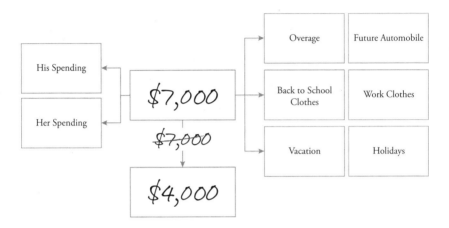

These days, she'll ask whether I want to go out for dinner, and I'll say, "Sure." So she'll ask whether I want to go to the hundred-dollar sushi place or to the Chick-fil-A three blocks down.

Of course, that's an easy question to answer if it's some sort of occasion or if I just want to treat her to a special dinner. But if it's night like any other, then I'm going to be more thoughtful about all of my other spending commitments. I'll ask, "Are you buying?"

She'll laugh. "Uh, no?"

"Okay then," I'll say. "Chick-fil-A it is."

Once a family splits up their accounts, it becomes easier to monitor individual lifestyle expenses—not just the short-term ones, but the long-term ones too. The overages. The gifts. The bills. The maintenance costs. The replacement costs. And once we started monitoring those expenses closely, we started to realize that we needed to allocate those resources in advance. Because if we didn't, our savings would disappear.

None of this is to say that you can't have nice things. In fact, just the opposite: it's precisely because we're you're careful that you're able to have such nice things.

Meanwhile, we're both putting aside the savings that we need to in order to grow ourselves, grow our finances, and grow the businesses that we own. We're accumulating wealth, preparing to make capital investments, and investing in our personal developments. We're reading, we're learning, we're growing. We're attending seminars. We're studying up—preparing for our future businesses and our future investments. By watching our spending and putting some energy toward forethought, we've managed to build a value-full life.

So remember: when you look at your account and see that you've got $7,000 set aside for lifestyle spending, you might not actually have $7,000 set aside for lifestyle spending. It might be more like $4,000. And that might sound a little sad at first. But it won't sound sad if you're being intentional.

It's good to make commitments with your lifestyle money. Make a commitment to pay off your mortgage. Make a commitment to pay off your car. Make a commitment to pay off your loans. Automatically pull that money out of your spending account every month. You might have a little less money to play with in the short term. But, in the long term, you'll have much, much more. You'll have real wealth.

IF YOU WERE WEALTHY, YOU WOULDN'T NEED TO SAVE

I know how hard this sounds. You have to set aside 30 percent of your income for savings. And on top of that, you have to factor all of these short and long-term spending commitments into your lifestyle budget. If it didn't sound hard to you, I'd be amazed.

I've worked with hundreds of entrepreneurs, doctors, dentists, and other professionals, and all of them say the same thing. They say that this 70/30 scheme is absurd, impractical, impossible. They say that I'm making sense *in theory*—they certainly agree that managing money this way would be nice—but they could never do it.

I hear this from people who make $20,000 a year, and I hear it from people who make $1 million a year. No matter who it is, they tell me they can't do it.

Of course, folks who earn more modest salaries reason that their reduced finances make saving particularly difficult. They figure that people with fancier jobs and bigger paychecks have it easier. "They've got more money," these clients say.

"Well, you know what?" I tell them, "They've also got more house."

I've never had someone say that the 70/30 split sounds easy. Even for doctors making half a million dollars a year, you tell them to allocate $400 a month toward mortgage payments and they say, "You want *what*?"

People seem to think that you need to achieve a certain level of wealth before you can start saving. But think about it: if you were wealthy, you wouldn't need to save. It's precisely because you *aren't* wealthy that you need to save. And while it sounds hard, it isn't really.

What makes saving difficult isn't your financial situation. It's your habits.

Implementing a new savings strategy sounds hard because we've gotten used to a certain kind of lifestyle. As we've become habituated to that lifestyle, we've started to consider the associated expenses normal—even necessary. And that goes for all of us—no matter what kind of a budget we're living on.

Remember the guy with "cash flow problems" who was spending $197,000 a month? When he told me that number, and I reflected back to him that most people would consider that figure astronomical, you know what his response was?

"You don't understand"—I swear, these were his exact words—"You don't understand," he said, "I'm from *Connecticut*."

To him, living in Connecticut meant not only that a certain kind of lifestyle was normal, but that it was *necessary*. You have to have five homes. You have to have five cars. You have to join these five country clubs. You have to, you have to, you have to.

The specific lifestyle expenses that he listed were certainly unusual, but his general argument was identical to the argument that I hear from all of my clients. In essence, his justifications were no different from the justifications that a person makes when they're earning $24,000 a year.

Both the modest earners and the high rollers end up saying the same things: there's no way to spend less, there's no way to accumulate, there's no way to save.

I hear this all the time. In fact, just three days ago, I met a doctor who's got a million-dollar practice. He was hoping that I could help him drive up revenues. So I gave him the whole spiel: you don't need to earn more, you need to save more.

"No can do," he says. "I can't possibly cut back."

"Why's that?" I ask. "You have a million-dollar practice, don't you?"

"Yeah," he says, "but I can't afford to save. I don't have enough money."

"How much are we talking?" I ask. "How much do you have?"

"Well," he says, "I've got three grand in the bank."

Three grand?

THREE GRAND!

You want to know how a doctor with a million-dollar practice ends up with only $3,000 in the bank? Well, when he came to see me, he flew first class, and he stayed in the Ritz-Carlton. You've got the beginnings of an answer right there. Saving isn't difficult for him because revenues are low. It's difficult because he's used to a certain kind of lifestyle—one that isn't financially sound.

Don't wait to earn more before you start applying the 70/30 principle. A bigger salary won't make things any easier. Whether we're earning thousands or earning millions, the work of saving money is equally difficult for all of us. It's also equally feasible for all of us. And equally transformative.

A friend and client of mine is a California-based orthodontist. Working together over the years, we've managed to turn his finances around in a big way. So he reached out to me a few months back and asked whether I'd be willing to meet with his daughter and her husband. His daughter's a schoolteacher, her husband's a mechanic,

> A bigger salary won't make things any easier. Whether we're earning thousands or earning millions, the work of saving money is equally difficult for all of us.

they've got a big mortgage, and they're worried about their finances. I said, absolutely—no charge. If they can get themselves down to Atlanta, I'll spend the day with them.

So I met with the couple, went over their finances, and introduced them to a number of wealth-building strategies including the 70/30 principle. By the time the day was out, we had a plan to pay off their home in twenty-four months, knock down their total debt to zero dollars, and start saving and accumulating $4,000 a month.

No part of that strategy involved ratcheting up their salaries to million-dollar or multimillion-dollar levels. These weren't investment bankers. They weren't Silicon Valley CEOs. They were a schoolteacher and a mechanic. And they already had everything they needed to start building wealth.

I know it sounds difficult. It might even sound impossible—saving 30 percent of your income every month. But if taxes went up 30 percent next year, you'd find a way, wouldn't you?

I'll tell you, I've used this 70/30 strategy with hundreds of clients, and I always check in with them twelve months later. I ask, "Did putting that money aside ever hurt you? Did it ever feel like a burden?" And I've never had a single person say that it did. I've never had anyone say that they were crushed or that they were living hand to mouth.

You know what I *have* had though? I've had people say that they thought this would never be possible, and that it turned out it was. I've had people say that their lives have never been better. That they're debt-free for the first time, saving for the first time. That for the first time in their lives, they feel like they're on the road to wealth.

———

EVERYTHING COMPOUNDS— FOR BETTER OR WORSE

We've talked a bit about the idea that philosophy matters. What you believe determines how you behave. Part of why that's true is because your philosophy determines what you value. It tells you what's worth measuring. And when we measure something, we give it attention. We work on it. And if we really focus and devote ourselves to working on something, we make progress. So whatever we measure, whatever we value—we get more of it.

Simply put: *You get what you measure.*

And the corollary: *You don't get what you don't measure.*

We saw the adverse effect of that principle toward the beginning of this chapter: If you measure income, you'll get more income, sure. But since you aren't measuring savings, you'll never save.

By contrast, once you start applying the 70/30 rule to your life, your measurements will change. You'll start measuring accumulation. You'll start measuring investment capital. You'll start measuring personal growth. And so you'll start getting more of all three. Because you get what you measure in this world.

When you're focused on twelve-packs, the main question you're going to ask is, *How can I buy more twelve-packs?* But once you start putting money into savings, once you start putting money toward future-investment funds, once you start putting money toward personal development, your questions are going to change. It'll be, *How do I accumulate more? How do I build more? How do I grow more?*

> As your questions start changing and your numbers start changing, *you* start changing.

As your questions start changing and your numbers start changing, *you* start changing. With less debt, more money, and a growth mindset, you're going to start feeling better. You're going to experience less stress and bring a different kind of energy to your relationships. Your friendships, your marriage—they're going to become stronger because you can give them more attention. And you're going to be bringing that same kind of heightened attention to your workplace too.

That's going to make your deliverables better, which is going to increase the value that you bring to your work. As we've seen, increasing the value of your work can have real dollar ramifications.

The changes that you're making are also going to affect the people around you, particularly if you share your experiences with them. The same way that we tell people about the movies that move us, the shows that move us, the albums that move us—if you start telling people about the books, seminars, and discoveries that move you, they're going to seek those things out too. They're going to start seeing the benefits of savings, accumulation, and personal development, and soon they're going to be sharing *their* discoveries with *you*.

So now you're not just reading about a better life. You're living it. You're telling others about it. You're seeing them live it and hearing about their experiences—the books that they're reading, the seminars that they're attending, the discoveries that they're making.

At a certain point, all of this has the compound effect of changing you for the better.

In the early days of their wealth journeys, Dreamers ask the wrong question. They ask, *How can I earn more?* The irony is that you can't answer that question by asking it. To answer that question, you need to ask a different question instead: *How should I manage that which I earn?*

Only once you start asking the right question—only once you start focusing on saving—will you start earning more. Because, as we've seen, saving changes your life—especially once you start putting 10 percent of your income toward personal development. You grow as a person. And growing as a person makes you more valuable to your organization. It makes you more valuable to the clients that your organization serves. And value yields money.

SAVER BEWARE TOO

I think some people hear about this stage of wealth development, recognize that they're in it, and become ashamed of that. *I'm just a Stage-One Dreamer,* they think.

But Stage One is incredibly powerful. Even with all of its pitfalls and frustrations—the low returns, the brutal grind, the overwhelming debt—it's still a stage to relish. Because Dreamers represent the best of us. They dream the biggest, they work the hardest, and they stand to grow the most.

What's unfortunate is that a Dreamer's ambition can become so powerful that it knocks them off course. In their eagerness to build and grow, the Dreamer becomes fixated on earnings and loses sight of the foundational work at the root of wealth development: savings and accumulation.

So that's where the 70/30 principle comes in—it sets the Dreamer back on track, helping them reach their goals.

But as powerful and as essential as the 70/30 principle is—as important as it is to save and accumulate—I have to warn you that accumulation can become a trap. You see, saving is a powerful tool, but it isn't powerful enough to deliver wealth all on its own. So if we're relying on savings, and savings alone, then we're setting ourselves up for disappointment, for disenchantment, for failure.

And that's the number-one biggest danger that you're going to face as you enter into Stage Two of your wealth journey.

STAGE TWO

2

THE
SETTLERS

IMAGINE THIS: You start a business. You put your heart and soul into it. And by sheer force of will, you make it successful. Meanwhile, you save diligently, stashing money away in investment accounts so that you can retire in style.

Then, one day, you feel like the time has come.

So you go to your financial advisor, and you let her know that you'd like to sell your business and file for social security. Your financial advisor looks at you, and then she looks at her computer.

She looks at you.

And then she looks at her computer.

Computer. You. Computer. You. Computer. You.

And she tells you that you can't retire.

You haven't saved enough, she says. You're going to have to keep working, she says. And maybe, just maybe, in five years or in ten years, you'll be able to retire, she says.

"Oh, and by the way," she says, "Happy birthday."

Because all of this is happening on the day that you turn seventy-seven.

Sound like a nightmare?

Well, believe it or not, I didn't dream this up. I witnessed it. During waking hours.

Jeff—we're going to call him Jeff—was a seventy-seven-year-old dentist who'd been working and saving for longer than most Americans have been alive. He'd accumulated $800,000 in savings—money that he'd handed over to his investment advisor for management. He'd also built a thriving business—his dental practice—and he owned the building that housed it.

One day, Jeff figures that seventy-seven is *old enough*. So he goes in to see his financial advisor and get the retirement ball rolling.

Unfortunately, it doesn't roll very far.

The financial advisor pulls out a calculator and walks Jeff through some simple math.

He's got $800,000 in the stock market.

Assuming a 5 percent return, that retirement fund will yield $40,000 a year, or a little less than $3,500 a month. Pretax.

Meanwhile, the mortgage payments on Jeff's building clock in at $7,300.

Which is to say that if Jeff retires today, his retirement fund won't be able cover even *half* of his monthly mortgage payments—let alone room, board, or any kind of a life.

"You can't retire," the advisor tells Jeff. "You haven't saved enough."

Happy birthday.

Flash-forward a few days and a friend of a friend of a client has put Jeff in touch with me. We're in my office now, and Jeff's at his wits' end. He says that he's seventy-seven years old. That he's been drilling teeth for more than fifty years. That he's pulled savings out of every paycheck he's ever gotten. And now he's being told that saving enough money to retire is a mathematical impossibility.

"I'm begging you," Jeff says. "Please, just tell me it isn't true."

So I look at the numbers, and I look at Jeff.

I look at the numbers. And I look at Jeff.

Numbers. Jeff. Numbers. Jeff. Numbers …

Jeff.

"I'm sorry, but it's true," I say. "You don't have time to save enough—not to retire the way you hoped."

YOU CAN'T SAVE YOUR WAY TO WEALTH

The journey to wealth begins with a dream. Or, for some of us, lots of dreams. The dream of building and supporting a family. The dream of building and growing a business. The dream of driving a certain car, owning a certain house, advancing a certain cause. Starting a foundation. Curing a disease. Traveling the world.

At the beginning of our journeys, we tend to fixate on income: we believe that if only we earned more, we could realize all of our dreams. And in the last chapter, we saw where that kind of thinking gets us: nowhere. We saw that *what you earn* matters a lot less than *how you spend it*. In short, we saw the power of saving.

But as powerful as saving is, it isn't *all*-powerful—and understanding that distinction can spell the difference between living out your wildest dreams and living out your worst nightmares. As Jeff unfortunately discovered.

For the better part of a half century, Jeff operated under the belief that he could save his way to wealth. And that belief became his undoing.

For all of us, there comes a time—perhaps it's at age seventy-seven, perhaps sooner—when we sit down, run the numbers, and discover the *limitations of accumulation*. We see that no matter how much money we stockpile, it will never be enough to make most of us wealthy. And that moment—the moment we realize that it is impossible to save our way to wealth—becomes a turning point.

It's not a good turning point for most of us—because most of us don't think to reject the notion of saving our way to wealth. Instead, we reject the notion of wealth itself. Or at least we redefine it, reducing it to match the size of our savings accounts.

It's with that compromise that we transform from Dreamers to Settlers—namely, people who've settled for a lesser kind of wealth.

> # When we retire, we tell our bodies that it's time to *stop*—that our lives are finished and that there's no work left to do.

So it's not with a bang but with a whimper that we begin Stage Two of our wealth journeys. We declare that our Stage-One dreams of upgrading our lifestyles weren't "practical," and that our plans to change the world weren't "realistic." We trade all of our early adulthood dreams away for one new one—a dream that's more *reasonable*, more *pragmatic*, more *achievable*: the dream of retirement. The dream that someday, we will be able to stop working, and live off our savings. The dream that we will then die before our savings run out.

And in most cases, wishing makes it so: with retirement comes a speedy death.

I don't mean that figuratively. Studies have shown that people who work longer live longer, and that those who retire earlier die earlier.[8]

It's no mystery why: retirement is a biological kill command. When we retire, we tell our bodies that it's time to *stop*—that our lives are finished and that there's no work left to do. And when you tell the body that it's time to stop, the body listens.

Medical practitioners call this the "Nocebo Effect," drawing on the Latin root "Noc," which means to harm. Or kill. Simply put, the Nocebo Effect is the mechanism whereby our negative beliefs cause real, measurable, physiological afflictions.

---

8   Wu, C., Odden, M. C., Fisher, G. G., et al. "Association of retirement age with mortality: a population-based longitudinal study among older adults in the USA." *Journal of Epidemiology and Community Health*, 2016.

One study compared two groups of people suffering from lung disease. Half of the test subjects believed that their astrological signs doomed them to die of their illnesses. The other half didn't share that belief. The study found that the patients who believed that they'd been born under a bad sign died, on average, *five years earlier* than their nonbelieving counterparts.[9]

In another case, a man tried to kill himself by overdosing on the experimental drugs that he had been given as part of an unrelated pharmaceutical study. After taking the pills, he nearly died. Doctors stabilized him and then evaluated his medication. They discovered that the man hadn't been given experimental drugs at all. He had been given placeboes. The only thing he'd overdosed on was the belief that he was overdosing—and it nearly killed him.[10]

My point is that *philosophy matters*. It's a fact. Verified by more double-blind studies than you or I could count. So if you adopt the belief that it's time to quit, your body will adopt that belief too.

Retirement is a death sentence. And the same is true when it comes to savings-oriented financial strategies.

If you think about it, the save-your-way-to-wealth strategy is a *stopping*-oriented strategy. Just as retirement is a stopping-oriented strategy. In the accumulation game, the goal is to acquire money and hoard it. Once we've earned the money, we don't want it to *go* anywhere. Just like, as retiring Settlers, *we* don't want to go anywhere.

When your money stops, it can't grow. Wealth becomes a mathematical impossibility. You're dead in the water.

So Stage Two of the wealth journey is defined by these twin fallacies: that retirement is the highest form of wealth, and that we

9   Madrigal, Alexis C. "The Dark Side of the Placebo Effect: When Intense Belief Kills." *The Atlantic.* September 14, 2011.

10   Reeves, Roy, and Ladner, Mark, et al. "Nocebo Effects with Antidepressant Clinical Drug Trial Placebos." *General Hospital Psychiatry*, 2007.

can achieve that wealth through savings. As we'll soon see, neither of those things are true.

But I also want to be clear here at the outset: I'm not saying that you shouldn't save. And I'm also not saying that you shouldn't retire. What I *am* saying is that there's more to wealth than savings, and that there's more to life than retirement.

That's precisely what this chapter is going to explore. Here we'll discover the difference between saving to horde and saving to spend. We'll discover the difference between retiring to stop and retiring to grow. And we will conclude with a vision forward—a plan for moving beyond Stage Two's save-to-retire philosophy, and toward Stage Three's earn-to-grow philosophy.

But before we get into any of that, I think it's best to begin by looking at the central fear that motivates us in Phase Two. It's the fear that prompts us to save compulsively, and the fear that defines most retirement plans. I'm talking about the fear that we'll run out of money before we die.

Where does that fear come from?

THE BUILD-A-BOGEY-MONSTER WORKSHOP

It's common to worry that we'll run out of money before we die. But, unless we're in dire straits, we generally don't worry that we'll run out of money *tomorrow*. Or next month. Or next year. Because tomorrow, and next month, and next year, we intend to be working. We intend to be earning an income.

There was once a time when people assumed that they'd *always* be working—that they'd *always* be earning an income. But that changed after 1935, when FDR signed the Social Security Act into law, establishing that American workers could expect to retire at age sixty-five.

Suddenly, there was a calendar date after which you could officially declare your intention to never earn an income again. And if your income was going to disappear, it would have to be replaced. Social security would cover some of that cost, but where would the rest of the money come from?

Enter Wall Street.

The finance industry took this beautiful idea—the right to retire—and weaponized it. Investment firms realized that they could use the national retirement age to create an artificial deadline by which every American would have to either achieve wealth or die penniless.

And it worked.

Today, retirement investment accounts are as universal as early-morning jogs, diamond-ring proposals, and bottled water. The finance industry has seen to that by doing what it does best: selling us stories.

And, if you're going to achieve wealth—*actual* wealth—it's crucial to understand this: the finance industry is *not* in the business of managing investor money. It's in the business of selling us stories. Just like every other industry.

I know because I used to be a part of it.

One of my earliest jobs in the financial industry was at one of the world's largest insurance and advisory firms. When I started there, I thought that an advisor's job would be to analyze

> The finance industry is *not* in the business of managing investor money. It's in the business of selling us stories.
> Just like every other industry.

market trends and recommend savvy trades. I'd look at stocks and bonds and help clients pick out the ones that would serve them best.

But that instinct was quickly corrected.

I was taught that the number-one job of a financial advisor isn't advising. *It's prospecting.* You want to know how most of the advisors I spent time with determined where to invest your money? They would look and see which mutual fund had the highest star rating. Then they would advise you to put your money there.

Literally—these advisors picked out mutual funds based on the number of stars they had next to their names. Like we were ordering Chinese food on Yelp.

Which isn't to say that financial advisors are lazy. In fact, just the opposite: they're some of the hardest-working people you'll ever meet. They're out in the field all day, running from meeting to meeting to meeting, working so hard to bring in clients that there simply isn't time for anything else. You've got to sign the client, stick them in mutual funds, and move on to the next lead.

And while five-star mutuals might sound pretty nice, the reality is that they usually aren't. The vast majority of the time, you're better off just indexing your money.

In 2007, Warren Buffett made a wager with the President and CIO of an asset management firm: Buffett would put $500,000 into an unmanaged index fund while the asset manager would put a matching sum into whatever he deemed to be the five most promising hedge funds on Wall Street. Then, they'd set a ten-year countdown clock and circle back when the buzzer went off. Winner take all.

A decade later, Buffett reported the results in his annual letter to investors. His opponent's favorite hedge funds had produced an average yield below 3 percent. One even went belly-up. The very best-performing fund had average annual gains of 6.5 percent.

And Buffett's unmanaged index fund?
It yielded 8.5 percent.

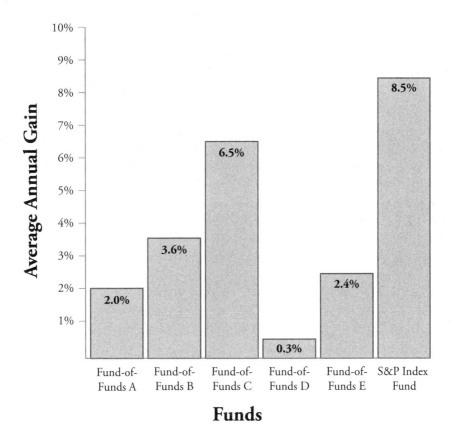

In his letter, Buffett pointed out that five hedge funds is *not* a small sample size. Each fund owned interests in more than two hundred other funds. Which meant that there were hundreds of elite investment professionals working on this bet.

And they still couldn't beat an unmanaged index. [11]

The Economist recently published a study that is, perhaps, even more damning. They took a look at all of America's top-quartile equity

---

11   Buffett, Warren. "Warren Buffett's Letters to Berkshire Shareholders." Berkshire-Hathaway.com, 2017.

funds from 2014 and tracked the performance of those funds over the following four years. After one year, 70 percent of those funds lost their top-quartile foothold. By 2016, fewer than 10 percent of those funds were still in the top quartile. And by 2017, none of them were. Not a single one.[12]

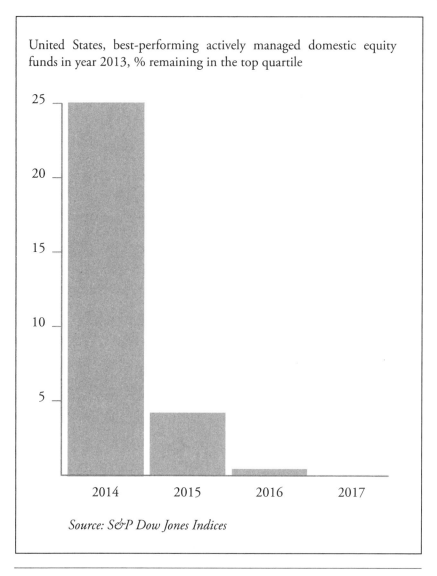

United States, best-performing actively managed domestic equity funds in year 2013, % remaining in the top quartile

Source: S&P Dow Jones Indices

---

12   "Troubles at the Woodford Investment Group Point to a Wider Trend." *The Economist.* June 6, 2019.

This is all by way of saying that financial advisors are great at what they're paid to do. But they the vast majority aren't paid to give you financial advice. They're paid to sign investors. That's true at Merrill Lynch, at J.P. Morgan, everywhere.

I recently had a client come in who had inherited a large sum of money when her father passed. She was planning to invest the new inheritance with her current advisor, but wanted to run the decision by me first.

When I looked at her portfolio, I saw that it wasn't doing well. She was down against the market, and she was paying big fees for the privilege. But instead of telling her to move the money, I simply encouraged her to get on the phone with her advisor and ask some basic questions—questions about fees, indexing, and the gap between her portfolio and overall market performance.

A few days later, she called me to report back.

"He couldn't answer any of the questions," she said. "He had to get a supervisor on the phone."

For years, she had been investing half a million dollars with this "investment advisor." And it turned out that he knew very little about investing.

These are the people who are encouraging us to save and accumulate.

At the individual level, I have a lot of compassion for these advisors: they're just trying to do their jobs—they're just trying to feed their families. But they can often do a great deal of damage in the process. Underinformed, undereducated advisors can unintentionally destroy their clients' financial futures.

In fact, 2008 taught us that they can destroy entire economies.

We always have to remember that *we get what we measure.* Our financial advisors aren't measured for quality advice. They aren't measured for portfolio performance. The main measurement that matters in their careers is *assets under management*. At the end of the quarter—at the end of the year—their employers will only be asking one question: *How much did you bring into the firm?*

Which is why you won't get much attention from most advisors if you aren't investing at least $1 million.

If you're investing $100,000, then your advisor is only going to earn about $500 a year off of your business. And they won't be making the slightest dent in their firm's total AUM. They simply won't be able to afford to think about you. Attention is a scarce resource, and they need to reserve it for their biggest investors.

Now, in defense of these advisors, the problem isn't that they *won't* help you if you don't invest more than $1 million. The problem is that many *can't* help you if you don't invest more than $1 million. Without a decent investment, many advisors would struggle even paying their own overhead.

As I have said, I am not here to beat up on financial advisors and have great respect for many of them. But I do want you to understand the model you are being placed in is not actual wealth and causes you to settle on the things you could accomplish in this lifetime.

For instance, let's look back at our friend Jeff.

What Jeff learned the hard way—and what we're about to learn the easy way—is that it's nearly mathematically impossible to generate a serious postretirement income from savings alone. Unless your savings are astronomical.

Math can't lie. It doesn't know how.

I know that, given the national narrative around retirement savings, this can be hard to believe. But I'm going to show you the math. And math can't lie. It doesn't know how.

MYTH VERSUS MATH

The save-to-retire myth goes something like this: The day that you turn sixty-five, you're going to want to stop working. Once you stop working, you won't have any more income. So you'll need to replace that money. Social Security won't help much—it may not even exist anymore—so you'll need to rely on savings. If you save enough, you'll be able to have the long, lavish retirement of your dreams. All you'll have to do is put that money into the stock market and live off the yield.

Can you spot the operative phrase?

It's "if you save enough."

If *retirement* is the bait, then *saving enough* is the catch. Because you can't. Our buddy Jeff saved diligently for more than fifty years, and that still wasn't enough.

Let's do some simple, round-numbers math to see for ourselves.

Imagine that you're currently living on an income of $50,000 a year, and you've got a retirement savings account worth $500,000. Assuming that the market never falters and that your portfolio reliably returns 5 percent, that "retirement fund" is going to be yielding $25,000 a year—before tax.

Relative to your current salary, that's a 50 percent pay cut.

Unless you were planning to adopt a ramen noodle diet in your sunset years, your new income probably isn't going to offer you the sort of lifestyle you'd hoped for.

Even if we double these numbers, it's still not looking good. Say you're used to living on $100,000, and you've got $1 million saved. Your retirement fund is going to yield you $50,000 a year—or $4,200 a month. Even if you saved $2 million and replaced your 100,000 income, that is money you can survive on, but it's certainly not wealth.

Therefore you will have to give up on so many of your dreams which is the whole point of this chapter and why becoming a Settler is so dangerous.

The numbers just don't typically add up. The vast majority of peoples retirement savings don't yield a high enough return to replace their preretirement income and create wealth. Not even close.

Remember that 50 percent pay cut, most retirees find it untenable. So every year, they dip into their principle a little to bridge the gap between their old income and their new one. But of course, that depletes their total savings. Which means that the following year, they're going to have less money in the market.

Let's go back to the million-dollar example. Our target income is $100,000 a year. We've got $1 million in savings. And that account is yielding $50,000 a year—or half of our target income.

Finding ourselves $50,000 short of our earning goal, we dip into our principal to make up the difference. Doing so means that we get $100,000 worth of spending money this year, just as we'd hoped. But it also means that our stack of retirement money is $50,000 shorter than it used to be. Since the principal just shrank, the next year's yield will shrink too.

In year two, we take home $47,500. So we dip back into our savings to make up the difference, pilfering even more this time. Last year we pulled out $50,000, and this year we're pulling out $52,500.

The upshot is that we're only two years into our retirement, and our savings account has already lost more than $100,000. From here, our losses will grow exponentially because every year, our principal will be smaller, and the gap between our desired income and actual income will be bigger .

If we weren't giving up on our dreams before, we sure are now. Factor in taxes, and our money won't last past our seventies.

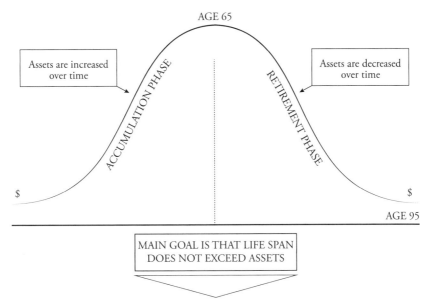

AGE 65

Assets are increased over time

Assets are decreased over time

ACCUMULATION PHASE

RETIREMENT PHASE

$

$

AGE 95

MAIN GOAL IS THAT LIFE SPAN
DOES NOT EXCEED ASSETS

Savings grow until retirement. Beginning with the first year of retirement, savings begin declining as we withdraw funds to cover lifestyle expenses.

Under this program, legacy, impact and long-term growth of assets, even after retirement, are not the main focus. They are typically set aside as aspirations (if there are enough assets left over), rather than being the main priority.

By the way, what is illustrated above is called "the death spiral," which most financial plans naturally put you in. If I never have the great pleasure of meeting you please make sure you never let someone put you in something called the "death spiral."

But this is what most financial plans naturally do. Don't believe me? Go back and look at the last financial plan an advisor gave you. It's often a bell-shaped curve with your assets going down every year until you pass away.

Also, it's because of this bell-shaped curve that the goal of most financial plans is that you don't outlive your money. That is the absolute definition of settling.

I can't imagine telling my kids that if they work really hard in this lifetime eventually they might be lucky enough to not outlive their money.

This is the irony of "fixed income": it's broken all over.

This is what a 401(k) buys you—what an IRA buys you. This is the promise you get in exchange for a lifetime of careful saving—in exchange for locking your money away for thirty or forty or fifty years—in exchange for depriving your family, your business, and yourself of capital. In exchange for all of that, you get an irrefutable, unbreakable mathematical guarantee that, in the example above, your income will drop by 50 percent on day one of retirement.

At the beginning of this chapter, we said that retirement tells your body to stop, and that stopping can literally kill you. Well, an accumulation-based strategy tells your finances the same thing, and they have the same reaction. The save-to-retire model is all about stopping the flow of money: you earn the money, you stick it in a shoebox, and you don't look at it again until you're sixty-five. And when you stop the movement of money like that, it dwindles and dies.

If your money doesn't move, it won't survive, and it certainly won't grow. Just like your body.

In a few pages, we'll look at an alternative approach—one that empowers your money to work and grow with you. But first, I want to return to this idea that stopping the body kills the body.

RETIREMENT VERSUS FREEDOM

I've said a few times now that retirement is a death sentence, so you'd be forgiven for thinking that I am entirely opposed to retirement. But actually, I'm not.

I think filing for social security is smart. And I'm all about creating time away from the office. Lots of it. In fact, that freedom—the freedom to step away from your job, your business, or your practice—is an essential component of my wealth philosophy. And it's precisely for that reason that I'm so vehemently opposed to retirement.

When I rail against "retirement," I'm not talking about the literal mechanics of retiring. I'm not talk about completing your SSA-1. I'm talking about the *culture* of retirement. I'm talking about the insidious idea that at age sixty-five, life rewards you with the opportunity to *stop*.

I've met people who truly believed that stopping was the ultimate form of wealth. They understood everything that we've talked about so far: they knew that their savings were going to disappear and that their income was going to get cut in half. And they just didn't care. They figured that it would be worth it: no more worries, no more work. They could sit and stare at the television from dawn to dusk and dusk to dawn.

For them, being thrifty wasn't a problem. Reducing their expenses wasn't a problem. As long as they could pay the cable bill.

They had settled. They had traded away all of their dreams in exchange for a new one: the dream of watching TV till they died—and dying before their money ran out. They'd made it to Stage Two of their wealth journeys, and that's as far as they wanted to go.

Go ahead and try talking sense to these people. All they do is tell you to shut your mouth: "Quiet," they say. "*Hannity*'s on!"

I suppose, if you know what you're getting yourself into and you're okay with it, then that's your prerogative. Go ahead and stop. Go ahead and burn your money. But if you're one of those people, then this book isn't for you. You probably should have figured that out way back in the introduction.

Remember when we looked at the three attitudes that people generally have about their lives? There was the *Poor Me* attitude, the *Leave Me* attitude, and the *Transform Me* attitude. I said right there in the intro that this book is for *Transform Me* types, not *Poor Me* or *Leave Me* types. And let me tell you: Settlers are textbook *Leave Me* types.

Leave Me is the entire foundation of the work-to-retire model. The ultimate goal is to be left alone—to be allowed to watch twenty-four-hour cable news in peace. These Settlers aren't interested in growing their wealth, in growing themselves, or in helping others to grow. They just want to *stop*.

And sometimes, that desire can become so fanatical that the Settler becomes utterly impervious to reason. To reality. To sense of any kind.

I recently met with a guy and talked him through the save-to-retire numbers—the same numbers we were just looking at. I was trying to show him that saving your way to a wealthy retirement is an arithmetical impossibility. And when I was done, you know what he said?

"I think your math is fuzzy."

That's all he had to say. *I think your math is fuzzy.*

Look—I'm a big believer in checking your advisors' math. I always tell people that they have no reason to trust me. And that they don't need to. As long as they trust math.

But this guy said my math was *fuzzy*, and I have absolutely no idea what that means.

Math can be right. Math can be wrong. But ask me. Ask Euclid. Ask anyone. Math cannot be *fuzzy*.

Did he think I was hitting the square root button by mistake?

Some people just can't bear to question the story that they've always been told—by their friends, by their family, by the culture around them. They'll stand by that story even if it requires them to declare that two and two is five.

This is why I find the *Leave Me* mentality to be the most problematic of the three. The *Poor Me* mentality is sad, sure. But the *Leave Me* mentality is worse. Seeing people put up blinders and deny the reality around them—that's more than sad. It's *scary*.

And a person can't honestly argue that Settlers don't have blinders up. The thing they want most in the world is security. It's control. And yet they adopt a financial strategy that absolutely guarantees a loss of control. When you're living on a fixed income, it's the *market* that has control. It's the pharmaceutical industry that has control. Your insurance has control. And you are at their mercy.

The only thing that a Settler controls is their television.

For the transformative personality, that's unacceptable. For them, the ultimate goal is *freedom*: the freedom to come and go as they please; the freedom to pursue their dreams without getting caught up in tight deadlines or tight purse strings.

Transformative types absolutely do dream of retirement too. But for them, retirement isn't about stopping. It's about *going*. Going anywhere, anytime, any which way they please. For this person, retirement isn't about staring at the walls—it's about scaling them: meeting challenges, forging legacies, and living the lifestyle they've always dreamed of.

Transformative personalities recognize that realizing their dreams means working. But not because they're working to earn or working to save. If your dream is to play the violin, if your dream is to sail around the world, if your dream is to create a charitable foundation, then you're going to have to work at it. You might even be working more than you ever have before. But you'll be working on your dreams. You'll be working on the things that you love.

Not to work means not to grow, and if you aren't growing you aren't living. We are meant to envision, to build, to create. Even in retirement. If we tell ourselves to *stop*—well, we've already seen studies that told us exactly what happens.

None of this is to say that transformative people can't relax. In my family, we have taken our kids on a vacation to Europe each year for the past few years—not for a few days, but for a few weeks. We can get away with that because we haven't spent our careers working toward retirement. Instead, we've spent them working toward *freedom*.

And that's what the rest of this chapter is going to explore: how to achieve freedom.

FINANCING FREEDOM

Freedom is a financial impossibility for Settlers because they're measuring accumulation. And to measure accumulation is to miss the point entirely. It's like playing chess to defend your pawns instead of playing to win.

Instead of measuring accumulation, we should be measuring financial freedom itself. We should be measuring the thing that we're trying to achieve.

What we mean by financial freedom is the freedom to give our time and attention to the things that matter most to us. It's the freedom to pursue our dreams without ever having to worry about money.

Now, finance academics don't call this "financial freedom." They call it "passive income." But it means the same thing: the money rolls in without you laboring for it, so you're free to pursue your dreams.

And that's what makes passive income so powerful: with a passive income, your labor doesn't earn you money—your assets do. Like clockwork.

What kind of assets?

Any kind.

Personally, my favorite assets are properties and enterprises: I like to buy and sell real estate, and I especially like to grow and sell businesses. After all, I'm an MBA. Building companies, running companies, growing companies—that's what I know. It's what I love.

> A stock portfolio is a means to an end, and nothing more. Like any other kind of asset, its job is to help you build passive income.

But it's not important that you acquire the same kinds of assets that I acquire. I've seen people generate passive income with stocks, with bonds, with commodities, you name it.

And this is important to clarify because I just spent a few pages tearing apart the 401(k)/IRA model. I'm not against 401(k)s, I'm not against IRAs, and I'm certainly not against the stock market. I think that you should have money ritualistically going into the stock market. I think you should dollar cost average. I think you should index.

We just need to be sure that we aren't letting our portfolios become ends in themselves. A stock portfolio is a means to an end, and nothing more. Like any other kind of asset, its job is to help you build passive income.

Personally, I put my savings in stocks so that I can grow those savings. Then I pull those grown savings out, and use them to acquire higher-yield assets, which contribute more to my passive income.

But I'm happy to endorse any kind of asset allocation strategy you can come up with, just so long as it's propelling you toward passive income. Toward financial freedom.

REVISITING THE 70/30 PRINCIPLE

In the last chapter, I made a big deal about the 70/30 principle. I said that if you're going to pursue wealth, you need to stop focusing on *earning* money, and start focusing on *managing* money. I said that you should set aside 70 percent of your income for lifestyle expenditures, and save the rest: 10 percent for wealth accumulation, 10 percent for capital investments, and 10 percent for personal development.

Now I'm saying that saving is a trap. I'm saying that the most important thing to do is buy up assets and grow your passive income.

So what's the deal? Am I contradicting myself?

Well, when we're at Stage One of our wealth journey, the biggest threat to our financial success is spending. If we don't get diligent about putting money aside, we'll never get anywhere. But saving is just one tactic. It's not the be-all-end-all.

What's more, the money that you save under the 70/30 principle isn't supposed to stagnate. It's supposed to work for you.

The most static tenth of your savings will the 10 percent that you put aside for wealth accumulation. That's money that absolutely does belong in a CD or an index fund. But even this "inert" money is working for you. First, it's giving you credibility in the eyes of the financial institutions that you might go to for strategic loans (which we'll talk about next chapter). And second, it's doubling as a rainy day fund—money you can always access in the event of a true emergency.

But that's only one-third of your savings. The rest of your savings are meant to be highly active.

Take, for instance, the 10 percent that you're setting aside for capital investments. You should be using this money to buy up income-yielding assets. This is money that you're putting to work, actively spending it in order to generate passive income. In a way, "savings" is a misnomer. What I mean when I call this money "savings" is that it's *earmarked*—not that it's locked away.

And finally, perhaps the most important, most active third of your savings is the 10 percent that goes toward your personal development. That, too, is money that you're meant to spend. If you're not spending it, you aren't following the 70/30 principle.

So while I do advocate for saving, I don't advocate for *stockpiling*. Our money shouldn't stop. We shouldn't be squirreling it away for some far-distant future—when we retire or when our grandchildren go to college. Instead, we save to spend. We save to grow, both personally and financially. We save, so that when opportunity comes knocking, we can answer the call.

It's not our savings that will make us wealthy. It's not our savings that will create impact. It's our passive income that will do that work.

A PASSIVE INCOME IN ACTION

The core principle of passive income is that you're not earning money with labor; you're earning money with assets. To illustrate how that works, I'm going to share approximate numbers from a recent acquisition that I was considering. This has become one of my favorite examples of a passive income asset, and in a moment, you'll see why.

I'm a wealth-building nerd, so I tend to spend my weekends doing some leisurely browsing for investment opportunities. One weekend, I happened to come across a condo listing pretty close to my house. The total asking price on this condo was $250,000. The down payment was $50,000. My expected earnings on one month of rent: $4,200.

To me, this was the kind of deal that passive incomes are made of.

The only cash I'd have to lay down out of pocket would be $50,000. And, by renting out the condo, I would recoup that down payment within a year. Within five years, the rent would pay off the mortgage too. And after that, all future rent money would be going directly into my pocket. I'd be earning $4,200 a month. $50,000 a year. Indefinitely. Just by holding onto an asset.

Do those numbers ring a bell by any chance? $4,200 a month? $50,000 a year?

Here's why I love this example so much.

If you flip back a few pages, you'll see that we got that exact same return when we were stashing our retirement savings on the market. Assuming no economic downturns and a consistently aggressive yield, we were going to earn $4,200 a month or $50,000 a year.

Besides for the volatility issue, there's just one tiny difference between earning that money via invested savings and earning it via this passive real estate income. And that tiny difference is $950,000 out of pocket.

To earn $50,000 a year from your invested retirement savings, you would need to first accumulate and invest *$1 million*. As we saw in the introduction, saving that sum would take most Americans *twenty years*.

And then comes along this condo, offering me exactly the same payout while requiring me to come up with just *one-twentieth* of the capital. Sure, $50,000 isn't nothing, but look at how much your family spends on cars. You can get your hands on $50,000. Certainly more easily than you can get your hands on $1 million.

Of course, getting your hands on $50,000 is going to be trickier if your money is locked up in an illiquid retirement account. You might not be able to access any capital at all. And that's going to be particularly problematic if you own—or plan to own—a business or practice.

Business owners need capital like painters need paint. If you don't have capital, you can't build a business. It's that simple.

Capital matters just as much to the mom-and-pop as to the *Fortune* 500. Sears and Toy "R" Us went belly-up for the same reason that your local independent pizza shop went belly-up: they ran out of capital. If you want your business to grow—heck, if you want your business to *survive*—the thing you need most is cash.

And you know what you're doing every time you put money into your IRA or 401(k)? You're giving away cash. Sure, you're giving it to yourself. But you're giving it to your *future* self, which, as far as the business owner is concerned, is pretty much like lighting that cash on fire.

As long as your cash is locked away as savings, you can't use it to grow your business. You can't use it to grow a passive income. You're effectively starving your business, locking away your capital for the next twenty to thirty years in exchange for the guarantee that your income will drop by 50 percent come retirement.

So why on earth would your investment advisor recommend this approach? Well, that depends. Are you cynical or generous?

If you're cynical, the answer is because your advisor can't make money off you when investing in your business. Their job isn't to help you get wealthy—it's to grow their firm's assets under management. So they need you to invest with them.

If you're generous, the answer is that they simply don't know better. Most financial advisors don't have an MBA. They're trained to work with W-2 employees, not business owners. They simply don't understand what you need. They don't understand how much they're hurting you or how much they're hurting your company. They don't know what it takes for a business owner to succeed.

Which reminds me.

Remember Jeff?

SAVING DR. JEFF

Let's review. At age seventy-seven, Jeff had $800,000 invested with his advisor. He also owned the building that housed his dental practice, and he was paying $7,300 a month to keep up with the mortgage. When he brought up retirement with his advisor, the advisor correctly explained that Jeff's $800,000 in savings would only yield him $40,000 a year on the market—less than half the cost of his mortgage.

After that meeting, Jeff panicked and came to me, begging me to tell him that his advisor was wrong. But I told him that his advisor was right: Jeff couldn't save enough money to retire.

And then I told him something else: I told him that this problem wasn't unique to him. I told him that saving to retire was a fool's game, and that most of us would never be able to manage it. I told him that if he wanted to retire, he'd have to do it by building a passive income stream. And I told him one more thing: I told him that he already had all the resources necessary to create that passive income. The only thing standing in his way was his *philosophy*.

When he asked me what the hell I was talking about, I responded by asking him how much he owed on his building.

"Four hundred thirty thousand dollars," he said.

"And remind me how much you have in savings?" I asked.

"Eight hundred thousand dollars," he said.

And then his eyes went wide.

It hadn't hit him until he'd said it out loud. Jeff already had everything he needed.

Two weeks later, he had his mortgage paid off. He'd sold his practice for a pretty penny, and, as part of the sale, he'd required the buyer to sign a ten-year lease on the building.

Now, instead of bleeding $7,300 a month in mortgage payments, Jeff was *earning* $7,300 a month in rent payments. He'd sold his practice, filed for social security, and—all told—created earnings of $120,000 a year. All in passive income.

That was three times more than he would have earned had he gone with his financial advisor's save-to-retire strategy. Under that strategy, Jeff would have needed to accumulate an additional *$2 million* in order to create the same income.

But hey, it shouldn't take Jeff more than forty years to save $2 million. And what's forty years to a seventy-seven-year-old?

———

WHAT YOU WANT, WHAT YOU NEED, AND HOW YOU'LL GET IT

So we've talked about the power of income-generating assets—and we've *seen* their power too. But, as we'll learn in the next chapter, it can be dangerous to go around buying up assets without any kind of agenda. It's important to develop a vision for how we plan to grow our income and what we're growing it for.

We won't find that vision in finance textbooks or in our investment advisor's office. We'll find that vision in our dreams.

Our journey toward wealth began with dreams, and those dreams will continue to guide us at every turn. Whenever we have doubts or uncertainties or hard choices to make, it's our dreams that will help us distinguish right from wrong. This is a lesson that I never stop relearning.

It wasn't so long ago that I met with a client—a woman who had just sold a $32 million company. We were meeting to determine the best way for her to manage that money moving forward.

Instead of starting with a risk assessment or searching for five-star mutual funds, I asked her a simple question: "What would you like your life to look like five years from now?"

So she started answering the question. She started telling me about the lifestyle she wanted to have and the legacy she wanted to leave behind, and, I don't know whether it was a minute later or ten minutes later, but at some point, I realized, with no small bit of shame and no small share of horror, that I hadn't been listening to a single word she was saying.

Because at some point during her answer, I realized that I had never explored this question for myself. I has asked all my clients, but I had never asked myself: What did I want *my* life to look like in five years?

> **We are more likely to succeed when we know what it is that we're trying to accomplish.**

This question is a crucial one to ask because the likelihood of achieving your goals is inordinately higher when you've defined what those goals are.[13] That should be obvious: of course, we are more likely to succeed when we know what it is that we're trying to accomplish. It's face-palm-level obvious. And yet somehow, I had never thought about it before.

In the years since, I've become more intentional about helping my clients develop and realize their visions for the future, and I've

---

13   "Study Focuses on Strategies for Achieving Goals, Resolutions." Dominican University of California, Dominican.edu.

also become more intentional about developing and realizing *my own* vision. In the process, I've developed two rules for setting long-term goals.

First: *Be thorough.*

"I want to be wealthy" isn't going to cut it. Neither will "I want to make an impact." Even "I want to put my kids through college" leaves us wanting for information. After all, paying for a state college and paying for a private one are two very differently priced cans of worms.

As you challenge yourself to be thorough, you'll discover how much you already know about the future you're dreaming of—and how much you have yet to learn. You'll also discover the surprising expenses that you'll have to plan for, as well as the areas in your life where you'll be happy to pay less for more value.

So get clear about the details. How often are you seeing your grandchildren? How often are you flying to Europe? On what airline, to what country, staying at what hotel? Do you have a personal trainer? Will you be fishing off the coast of Costa Rica, or will you be fishing off the coast of Sicily? Those are two very different things. How many cars do you have? What kind? Who's driving them? Oh and that lake house you live in—are the shingles asphalt, slate, or solar?

The more you know about your vision for the future, the easier it will be to follow the next rule.

And here's the next rule: *Be honest.*

Once you know the kind of life you want to lead, it's time to figure out what it's going to cost. Namely, just how much passive income are you going to need to generate? How much money will it take for you to feel that it is inconsequential whether you do or don't work? *Be honest.*

A year ago, I sat down with a couple and asked them to tell me their number: How much passive income would they need to live the life of their dreams?

The wife said they would need ten grand a month.

I let that proposal hang in the air for a moment, and then I said, "Okay, great. Now tell me the real number."

She laughed and said it was $50,000 a month.

She seemed to believe that $50,000 was too much to ask for. It felt scary for her to say the real number out loud. But there's no need to be afraid. As long as you know what you're targeting, you can achieve it.

Be thorough. Be honest. And build outward from there.

———

SETTLERS NO MORE

Once you have a clear path, all that's left to do is pursue it. Evaluate what money you already have coming in, consider how much you'd *like* to have coming in, and determine what you'll need to do in order to bridge that gap.

> Growing a passive income is much more efficient than saving your way to wealth.

Unlike the Dreamer at Stage One and the Settler at Stage Two, you're not going to be focusing on driving up your wages, and you're not just going to be saving. You're going to use your earnings to acquire assets, which will then yield passive income—income that will make it possible for you to focus less on laboring and more on growing.

Determine what steps you can take to systematically increase your passive cash flow every year. For instance, you might already have stocks. You might have real estate. You might have a business that doesn't require you to be around all the time. Those are all passive income sources that you can scale. And what you don't have yet, you can start acquiring and building.

From there, you'll want to get clear about how many years it's going to take for you to achieve your target cash flow. What you'll discover is that growing a passive income is much more efficient than saving your way to wealth.

You'll also unlock new degrees of power with respect to the Compound Effect. You'll see how acquiring assets and growing passive income unlocks opportunities to acquire *more* assets and grow *more* passive income. And as your resources grow, your dreams will grow too.

To help me stay on track, I find it helpful to create a simple *T*-shaped grid, labeling one side "Closer" and one side "Further." Then, every time I'm faced with an opportunity, I simply look at that grid and ask myself, "Will this move me closer to my goals or further away?"

The beautiful thing about this is that I don't second-guess myself anymore. I don't have to think things through forty different ways. If an opportunity will move me closer, I take it. If not, I don't.

This simple process of creating a vision, mapping it to a *T*-grid, and consulting that grid on decisions has changed my life. I've excised everything that was getting me further away from the life that I wanted—the bad habits, the toxic relationships, the dead-end work. And anything that could get me closer, I've developed and dialed up: good habits, inspiring friendships, and transformative work.

VISION MAPPING

Goals	CLOSER	FURTHER

With a thorough, honest vision, and a t-grid to guide me, I managed to achieve everything on my list within just seventeen months.

So much for a five-year plan.

Now that list of things that I'd like to achieve continues to grow every day. And, as a consequence, so do I.

It's this notion of continuous growth that will propel us into Stage Three of our journey. Where Stage Two was designed for depletion, Stage Three is designed for growth. Where Stage Two trends downward, Stage Three trends upward.

In Stage Two, the idea was that I would someday retire and never have to work again. I would live off my accumulated savings, which would dwindle, dwindle, dwindle without cease, and I would hopefully die before the money ran out.

By contrast, in Stage Three, the idea is that your assets and income should never stop growing.

That distinction becomes particularly vivid in down markets.

For the Stage-Two Settler, a down market is a catastrophe. I watch my 401(k) drop 40 percent, and I freak out. I wonder whether I'll ever be able to retire. I worry that I might never be able to stop working.

Meanwhile, as a Stage-Three thinker, you see a market collapse as a golden opportunity. By building up your capital investment savings, you've positioned yourself to take advantage of the down market. While everybody else contracts, you expand. While everybody else pulls back, you lean in. When everyone else sells, you buy. To you, the down market is just one big fire sale.

As Settlers, we learn an important lesson: we learn about the power of savings. But that lesson comes at a terrible cost. We buy into a narrative that saving is the only way to wealth, that our dreams are impractical, and that the only kind of bliss we can expect is the bliss of a life without work. Where once we had high hopes, now we are left with a single fear: that we will outlive our money. And so the save-to-retire model is born.

The save-to-retire model offers a compelling narrative, which is why large financial institutions have been so successful selling it to us. But that's all the save-to-retire model offers: a compelling narrative. The reality it is nearly impossible to save your way to wealth, and as we have seen an extremely inefficient use of dollars. And even if you could save your way to wealth, your wealth wouldn't do you any good—not if all you wanted to do with your life was *stop*.

Retirement is a beautiful thing. But not when it's about stopping. Not when it's about staring at walls. Instead, a true retirement orients itself toward growth. It gives you the freedom to realize your dreams.

The engine that drives such a retirement is a passive income. By acquiring assets that appreciate, you can build a passive income that snowballs, growing larger all the time, and empowering you to pursue and achieve your dreams—dreams of a larger lifestyle, a longer legacy, and an impact that you can be proud of.

From there, there's only one thing left that can get in your way. And we'll look at it in the next chapter.

It's called Ego.

STAGE THREE

3

THE
RISK TAKERS

IT'S TOWARD THE BEGINNING of my career. My office is situated on the grounds of a high-end country club, and from my desk, I can see the golf course: ponds, trees, sand traps—all of it. What the club members call *hazards*, I call *one heck of a view*.

I can also see the members themselves. They dress well, they drive nice cars, they golf all day long, but most of them are barely solvent. I know because I'm a junior mortgage officer. When these club members buy houses, I'm the one reviewing their loans. I'm the one looking at their W-2s and their bank statements and their credit reports. And I can see right there on paper that while they're all living larger than I am, they're actually not much richer than I am. They might have lots and lots of money coming in, but that money isn't really theirs. It belongs to the bank. These people are as overleveraged as can be. Their debt-to-income ratios are downright nauseating.

At this stage of my life, I don't yet know what wealth is, but I sure as heck know what it isn't. And I estimate that there's not a single dues-paying member of this club whom you could honestly call wealthy.

Until, one day, I meet one.

I meet two, in fact.

It's a couple unlike all the rest. I know that they're aged around sixty or sixty-five, but they seem like the youngest people I've ever met—kissing, smacking each other's butts. You might remember these folks. We met them back in Stage One. To this day, I think of them as one of the happiest couples I've ever met. We'll call them the Langs.

I pull up their W-2s, and I see that neither of them has ever been salaried above $30,000 a year. Which is strange because the couple's bank statements put their liquid assets north of $30 million.

I figure that whatever wealth is, these lovebirds have got it.

So I dig around inside their paperwork looking for some answers. How did their lives get to be like this? Where did all this money come from? I dig, and I dig, and I dig, and eventually it becomes clear that I'm not going to get answers from their paperwork. If I want to know, I'm just going to have to ask.

So I do. And they tell me.

When they first married back in the seventies, the Langs got themselves a home and a mortgage just like everyone else they knew. But unlike everyone else they knew, the Langs were discomfited by their mortgage. Owing money made them uneasy. They didn't have a whole lot of salary coming in, and they worried that they might never manage to pay off the house.

So they decided to make home ownership—*true* home ownership—a priority. Come hell or high water, they were going to pay off that mortgage. And fast.

They became intentional about living within their means, about saving, about putting money toward their mortgage. And within just a few years, they had it paid off. The house was theirs. All theirs.

With the mortgage gone, there weren't any big bills left to pay. The Langs could have adopted a more lavish lifestyle—they could have lived a little larger and still made ends meet. But now they were accustomed to living modestly. They figured that instead of changing their lifestyle, they could continue living humbly and putting money aside.

The difference was that this money wouldn't go toward mortgage payments. It would go toward savings.

A few years later, housing prices dropped, and the Langs got a brainwave. Paying off their mortgage had taught them that by carefully managing their money, they could handle debt at a strategic level. Meanwhile, they'd managed to save up quite a lot of cash, and they knew they didn't want it wasting away under their mattress. They wanted to put those dollars to work.

So they did some research and found themselves a condo in Florida—one that had seen a 30 percent price drop since the decline of the housing market. And they bought it.

It wasn't an impulse purchase. It wasn't a lifestyle purchase. It was an investment in their first-ever passive-income-yielding asset.

While the housing market was down, that Florida condo yielded rent—rent which first went toward paying off the mortgage, and then, eventually, went into Lang family pockets.

And then the housing market recovered. The value of their properties skyrocketed. The Langs sold their personal home, they sold their Florida condo, and they raked in massive profits on both.

Then, instead of spending those profits on a mansion, the Langs made a radical decision: they decided to keep doing what they were doing. They decided to continue living within their means, continue saving, and continue investing. Using their huge stash of earnings, the Langs moved into another modest home, and held onto the surplus for a future investment.

The next time housing prices dropped, the Langs bought up more real estate. A lot more real estate. And they followed the same cycle. They used the down years to acquire properties while enjoying passive income from rent payments, and they used the up years to sell and collect capital.

By living modestly, they were able to stay out of personal debt. And by putting passive rent income toward mortgages, they were able to stay out of investment debt too.

It took a great deal of discipline, but that discipline paid off. Soon, a couple who had never earned a combined income higher than

$60,000 found that they worth ten, fifteen, twenty, and eventually thirty million dollars.

"So," Mrs. Lang said, "That's our story."

I signed them to a new mortgage—one that I felt sure they would pay off in a matter of months—and that was that.

As far as the Langs were concerned.

But for me, that wasn't that at all. Their story stuck with me for the rest of the day, for the rest of the week, for months, for years, for a decade and more.

In those first few months after meeting them, I felt sure that the Langs had found the ultimate strategy for growing wealth. I felt sure that to become successful, I'd have to master the real estate market just as they had.

But over the decade that followed, as I devoted my career to investigating the nature of wealth, it became clear that the Langs' specific strategy was beside the point. What made them wealthy wasn't their approach to buying and selling residential homes. What made them wealthy was their *philosophy.*

The Langs couldn't possibly have achieved so much so fast if they had been fixated on Stage-One or Stage-Two notions of wealth. Had they approached real estate from a Stage-One mindset, they would have been so fixated on the income that their properties generated that they wouldn't have noticed the debt that they were accumulating to pay for those properties. And they wouldn't have saved a penny either. They would have allowed their spending to grow with their income, creating net gains of nothing at all.

Likewise, had they approached their successes with Stage-Two thinking, their passive income would never have grown. Once they'd gotten their first house paid off, they'd have put all of their savings into 401(k)s and IRAs, where the capital would have withered and died—as we saw in the previous chapter.

The Langs were able to create wealth because of their philosophy. They understood that *assets are greater than income.*

Assets are greater than income.

Early on, the Langs discovered that assets create passive income, and that they could put that passive income toward the acquisition of additional assets, which would, in turn, produce more passive income. To be successful, all they had to do was keep debt low and live within their means.

As we'll soon see, the Langs represent Stage-Three thinking at its finest. It's a stage defined by its focus on passive earning and aggressive acquiring. The Langs were able to leverage those strategies to create extraordinary wealth.

But, like I said, the Langs represent Stage-Three thinking *at its finest.* There's also a dark side to Stage Three, and that dark side begins and ends with ego. Many Stage-Three thinkers see their incomes growing, see their coffers filling, and they become reckless. They borrow too much, acquire too quickly, and lose sight of the fundamental Newtonian truth that what goes up must come down.

It's for this reason that I describe Stage-Three thinkers as "Risk Takers."

In time we'll see that effectively leveraging the power of Stage Three requires discipline, savvy, and humility. It requires us to become thoughtful about debt, about strategic relationships, and about market cycles.

For the Langs, what first inspired their transition to Stage Three was their discovery that the housing market would regularly bubble up and burst. Which is to say that, for them, their journey to wealth began with their discovery of market cycles.

So that's where we'll begin as well.

————

RISKY BUSINESS

Meet "Chris." Here he is now, his cherry-red Ferrari screeching to a halt outside Ohio's Muirfield Village.

This is where he lives: a miniature city built to serve uberwealthy golfing pros and their uberwealthy fans. Chris may or may not be one of these golf aficionados himself; in all the time I knew him, I never saw him swing a club. So he might be a golfer or he might not be—I don't know. What I do know is that living here gives him a certain kind of status. And status is something that Chris cherishes. It's what he sells.

Chris is a nationally renowned real estate guru, revered for his books, CDs, seminars, and lavish lifestyle. Pay him big bucks, and he'll teach you how to get a big loan, how to buy a big house, how to fix it, and how to flip it for a prodigious profit. Personally, he's got fourteen apartment buildings and $50 million in cash.

Real estate's his game, and he's got it all figured out.

The year?

2007.

————

It's the biggest cliché in finance.

It's the very first thing we learn about investing.

It's the golden rule.

Buy low. Sell high.

We all know it, and yet so few of us follow it. So many of us look at market bubbles and see buying opportunities. Then, when the bubbles burst, we sell.

It would be nice if we could chalk that up to inexperience, but the reality is that some of the biggest offenders are also among the biggest players. They're the best-financed, most experienced investors among us: the hedge fund managers, the mega-bankers, the real estate gurus.

These are people who've made it past Stage Two on their wealth journey. They've learned that assets are more powerful than income. They've enjoyed tremendous success buying and selling those assets. And then they've allowed that success to go to their heads. They've allowed themselves to believe that they've mastered the market—that they'll never be vulnerable to another downturn. And in that hubris, they've come to see up markets as buying opportunities—as forums for expansion.

Desperate for investing capital and certain of their prospects for success, these Stage-Three Risk Takers overload on debt and purchase assets at inflated prices. Then, when the passive income comes rolling in from those assets, these Risk Takers don't bother paying down their debt. After all, what's the rush when things are going so well? Instead, they use their winnings to acquire more assets.

To be fair, it's worth noting that many Risk Takers are trying to be responsible—they're just doing it wrong. They use their passive income to acquire additional passive-income-yielding holdings. They're buying up promising assets, just as they should. The trouble is that they're buying more of these assets than they can really afford. And at outlandish prices.

Meanwhile, the less responsible Risk Takers put off loan payments in order to acquire more *stuff*. Cars. Jewelry. Homes. Astronomically expensive club memberships. Not only do these assets not appreciate—they actually *depreciate*. But that doesn't faze these Risk Takers. Their egos have taken over.

These spendthrifts can't imagine a future in which values aren't going up. So they're disregarding their debts. And the banks are very happy to let them do just that.

In fact, banks reward these borrowers by signing them for even more loans.

> It turns out that we're not going to see continuous growth from now to eternity. Eventually the bubble bursts and the market crashes.

You see, the banks are making exactly the same mistake. They're behaving like nothing will ever change—like we'll be seeing continuous growth from now to eternity.

And then, of course, it turns out that we're not going to see continuous growth from now to eternity. Eventually the bubble bursts and the market crashes.

And how do our Risk Takers react?

They sell. They contract. Business owners print pink slips. Investors short. And real estate gurus go bankrupt.

The moment the housing bubble burst, it became clear that while Chris may have been rich, he had never been *wealthy*. He'd financed his real estate ventures with borrowed capital, and he'd never gotten around to paying back any of those loans—not because he couldn't afford to, but because he didn't see any reason why he should. He figured that the market would be booming forever, so why worry? He could buy a Ferrari now, buy a mansion now, buy fourteen apartment buildings now, and pay his loans back later.

Well, he did pay later.

After 2008, he lost his Ferrari. He lost his mansion. He lost his fourteen apartment buildings. All of it. Gone. And the same went for his son.

For years, Chris had been supporting his son—a son who'd managed to marry, acquire three luxury cars, and move into a mansion without ever learning to care for himself. When Chris went bankrupt, his son lost his cars, his home, and his marriage.

Back in Stage One, we saw that the Compound Effect cuts both ways—the investments that you make in yourself snowball, and the failure to invest in yourself can snowball too. Well, the same goes for our legacies: they cut both ways. If we're hungry, humble, and smart, we can transmit a legacy of wealth to our children. And if we're greedy, arrogant, and foolish, we transmit a legacy of poverty—or, at the very least, one of struggle.

Chris never forgave himself for initiating his son into a tradition of reckless acquisition—a tradition that ultimately ended in bankruptcy. Ultimately, Chris came to regret it all: what he'd done to his son and what he'd done to himself.

The last time I saw Chris was in 2009. He was in one of his tenants' units, sweating through his shirt, repairing a stove in hundred-degree weather.

He wasn't a real estate guru anymore. He was a glorified property manager.

THE POWER OF PESSIMISM

The central problem of Stage Three is that the power goes to our heads. We see the power of our assets, and it enthralls us—much as the power of our savings enthralled us back in Stage Two.

In a way, Stage Three is an overreaction to Stage Two. We bounce back, but too far. Where before, *fear* consumed us, now it's *overconfidence* that undermines our success. The ego takes over. We take risks that we ought not to, acquiring assets left and right without any kind of a strategy. And all too often, we finance those acquisitions with debt.

When we do, we effectively revert back to Stage One of our wealth journey.

In the first chapter of this book, I said that the Dreamer is always at risk of becoming too focused on income—that bringing more money in doesn't help if you're not *keeping* any of it. I said that as income rises, spending rises too—so with Stage-One thinking, you never get any wealthier.

And then, at the end of chapter two, I seemed to make the opposite claim: I said that income is the answer to everything. I suggested that you can't get wealthy unless you're measuring your passive income. I said that savings are a trap and that passive income is the holy grail of wealth-building.

I wonder: did those two chapters sound contradictory to you? I wouldn't blame you if they did. The first chapter warns against measuring income and the second advocates for it. That sure *sounds* contradictory.

But it isn't really.

If you look at Chris's story, and if you look at the Langs' story, you'll see why.

At first glance, Chris seemed to be pursuing the same financial strategy that the Langs pursued. He was buying up high-value properties in order to generate wealth. And, as I said at the beginning of this chapter, that is absolutely the key to getting past Stage Two: you have to learn to put assets ahead of income.

The difference is that Chris never really *owned* any of his assets. He may have had $50 million in the bank, but he had twice as much in debt. Which means that the *bank* owned Chris's properties. All Chris owned was the passive income itself.

Even though Chris wasn't a traditional Stage-One Dreamer—he wasn't focused on measuring salary earnings or business revenues—he still was focused on measuring income. Namely, *passive* income. And for that reason, he was never able to achieve wealth.

> Assets can only create wealth when they are acquired strategically— with humility.

The successful Stage-Three thinker understands that it's not just the passive income, but also the assets themselves, that create wealth. And this thinker also understands that assets can only create wealth when they are acquired strategically—with humility.

One key way to practice that humility is by performing what I call *Pessimistic Modeling*.

As we saw above, the Risk Taker assumes that market bubbles will last forever. So when the market's up, they borrow capital and acquire like crazy. Then, when the market collapses, they panic. They sell to survive.

Pessimistic Modeling is a tool that protects Stage Three thinkers from falling into this trap.

Pessimistic Modeling is a variation on the standard practice of Economic Modeling. Economic Modeling is the process by which we evaluate the market's possible futures and use that evaluation to inform our present-day buying and selling strategies.

The essence of the Risk Taker's mistake is that they only practice *optimistic* Economic Modeling. The only possible future that a Risk Taker evaluates is one in which prices will continue to climb. As a Risk Taker, I figure that if the economy is going to keep on roaring for the next five years, then I may as well keep on buying.

And that isn't exactly wrong.

If the economy is indeed going to keep on roaring for the next five years, I should absolutely keep on buying. But Pessimistic Modeling reminds me that the economy might not continue booming at all. In fact, it might collapse.

To perform Pessimistic Modeling, all you have to do is ask yourself: What if the stock market drops 40 percent tomorrow? What if the real estate market tanks? What if the next Congress raises taxes by 20 percent? What if you become sick or injured? What if you become so sick or injured that you can't go into work or manage your business? Or what if you simply lose your job?

Pessimistic Modeling doesn't require complicated math. It doesn't require us to dig up our old calculus textbooks. It simply requires us to exercise a little humility—to entertain the possibility that we might not have it all figured out—that we might be surprised by sudden downturns.

By doing some Pessimistic Modeling, we can prepare ourselves for the worst, even as we continue hoping for the best. We can protect our assets and ourselves, ensuring that, if the economy tanks, we won't tank with it.

In fact, the most effective Pessimistic Modelers pursue strategies that empower them to *expand* during down markets. After all, that's the first half of the golden rule, isn't it? Buy low.

When the market's down, that's when you want to buy stock, buy property, buy a business—because everything's on discount. This is also when the business owner wants to launch their most aggressive marketing strategies and increase production: competition's scarce in down economies.

When everybody else contracts, you expand. When everybody else pulls back, you lean in. When everybody else is freaking out—well, so are you. Because this is the opportunity of a lifetime.

> When everybody else contracts, you expand. When everybody else pulls back, you lean in.

This was the brilliance of the famed John Templeton. Or, *Sir* John Templeton, I should say. While his peers invested in what were supposedly "sure-thing" growth stocks, Templeton invested where prospects seemed gloomiest. He put oodles of money into low-cost value stocks and made oodles of money in the process. When he sold his investment firm in 1992, it was worth $13 billion.[14]

This is how the wealthiest among us *became* the wealthiest among us: they invested in down markets.

And we can do the same.

All we need is a little capital.

---

14   Chen, James. "Sir John Templeton." Investopedia.com. June 25, 2019.

GETTING OUR HANDS ON CAPITAL

The more we perform Pessimistic Modeling, the more we appreciate the power of the 70/30 principle—particularly with respect to saving 10 percent of our income for accumulation and saving 10 percent for capital investments.

The money that we save for accumulation is there to protect us during these bubble bursts that our Pessimistic Modeling predicts. It's there so that if there's a market crash, or an act of God, or if I suffer some sort of personal injury, I have the resources to continue caring for myself and for my family.

> The bright side of down markets is that everything's on sale.

And whereas that first 10 percent protects us from the dark side of down markets, the second 10 percent empowers us to take advantage of the bright side.

The bright side of down markets is that everything's on sale. It's a buyer's market. And the only thing that you need to have in order to take advantage of that buyer's market is a bundle of cash. That's why you've been earmarking 10 percent of your savings as capital investment money: so that when a down market strikes, you can strike back.

But saving money isn't the only way to collect capital. The money that we make by *selling high* shouldn't all become leisure money. We saw how that approach played out for Chris. Instead, we should be repurposing our profits as capital for future investments.

Both of these capital-securing strategies—saving a portion of our passive income and recycling sales profits into future investments—require us to live within our means. Just look at the Langs: they could have taken their first big windfall and blown it all on a mansion for themselves, but instead they decided to keep their lifestyle spending constant. Instead of spending their profits on fancy *stuff*, they repurposed those profits as capital, acquiring more assets in the next down market and effectively compounding their money.

They also made a point of keeping personal debt to a minimum, ensuring that they could put all of their savings toward future investments while preventing themselves from becoming overleveraged. That meant that they never spent more than 70 percent of their income on lifestyle purchases. They didn't go into credit card debt in order to finance shopping habits, and they didn't buy lots of cars with lots of loans.

Paying off personal debt and keeping it low can require us to make sacrifices, but they're sacrifices that pay off. I once had a client tell me that she would do whatever it took to pay off her student loans. These were the kind of loans that most people take twenty or thirty years to pay off. But she wanted to pay them off in half that time.

"I'll eat peanut butter sandwiches if I have to," she said.

So she put herself on a shoestring budget. And, when all was said and done, she had her loans paid off within just *sixteen months*.

Today, she's one of the wealthiest people I know.

And she's just getting started.

In the short term, living within our means can feel restrictive and burdensome. But doing so frees us of debt. It allows us to put our money toward investments and ensure that we'll be living large down the road. Just look at that client who paid off her student loans. Look at the Langs. Today, these people have more money than they know what to do with.

WHAT MAKES "STRATEGIC DEBT" STRATEGIC?

When I caution people about personal debt, many respond by asking about strategic debt. Surely, they suppose, it's okay to take on debt if the debt's being used to build a business or acquire an asset.

For those who aren't familiar, *strategic debt* is another means by which we can secure investment capital. It's debt that you take on in order to buy and build high-yield assets—assets that will ultimately earn you more in passive income than you'll spend in loan payments. It's justified debt. Acceptable debt. Sometimes even *smart* debt.

Strategic debt is a powerful tool. Which means that, like any other power tool, it can kill us if we mishandle it.

Most people think that as long as they're using their debt to buy up passive-income-yielding assets, then the debt qualifies as "strategic debt." But we don't determine whether a loan is strategic based on how we plan to spend the money. We determine whether it's strategic based on how we plan to pay it back.

All debt is debt—even debt that you use to acquire high-yield assets. It only becomes strategic when you put a concrete repayment plan into place. If you don't have a concrete repayment plan—if you allow the debt to fester—it will become a plague on your business, your family, and yourself. And it could ultimately wipe you out.

The biggest financial collapses are never caused by personal debt. They're caused by strategic debt—strategic debt that wasn't ever really strategic.

Look at our buddy Chris. Chris seemed like he was being responsible. He never borrowed money to buy fancy cars or gold watches or three-hundred-dollar bottles of wine. He only borrowed money when it would position him to acquire big, luxury apartment buildings—properties that all-but-guaranteed him massive ROI.

The problem is that he then used all of that ROI to buy fancy cars and gold watches and three-hundred-dollar bottles of wine. He never put that money toward paying back his loans. Which is to say that his debt never became strategic. So he ended up disastrously overleveraged and got completely destroyed by the '08 market crash.

Chris's debts could have been strategic—if only he had given more attention to paying them back.

I recently met with a dentist who wanted to build a new operatory for her practice, but she knew that building it was going to cost her $60,000—money she didn't have. So she came to me asking whether she ought to borrow the money.

"Well, how much do you think this new operatory is going to yield?" I asked her.

She said that it would bring an additional $10,000 of free cash flow into her practice every month.

So I said that she absolutely should borrow the money—just so long as she was prepared to get strategic about repayment.

If she takes that $10,000 a month and puts it toward renovating her house—or even if she puts it toward something that's ostensibly responsible, like hiring a new team member—then her $60,000 of debt is going to fester. It's going to canker. And it's ultimately going to cause serious damage to her practice.

But if she's strategic—if she puts that new $10,000 a month toward paying down her debt—she can have the $60,000 loan paid off in just six months. And then she'll have an extra $10,000 coming into her practice every month—indefinitely. *Then* she can renovate her house or expand her team or do whatever she wants to do with that new passive income.

Strategic debt can be a great tool for generating additional investment capital. You just have to be sure that it's actually strategic.

CALCULATED RISKS

> Every acquisition, every investment, every dollar spent is a risk. And it's precisely those risks that make us successful.

So far in this chapter, we've spoken a lot about the importance of proceeding with caution. We've seen that we always have to be planning for the worst. We've seen that we have to save and live within our means and never take on debt that we don't have clear plans for repaying.

My goal so far has been to drill home that we can't afford to have our egos to take over. Purchasing new assets is smart, but not when those purchases put us at risk of losing everything.

Still, it's important to clarify that risk isn't all bad. Risk is a cornerstone of entrepreneurialism. Sometimes, you have to take a leap. Sometimes you have to go out on a limb. If you don't, you'll never be able to test the boundaries of what's possible.

That's true, first and foremost, on a personal level: asking that woman for her number, telling that guy that you love him, getting on one knee, saying *I Do*, starting a family—each and every one of these things is a risk. They're the risks that make life worth living.

Wealth-building works the same way. It's a risk to quit your dead-end job. It's a risk to start your business. It's a risk to say that you're going to set aside 30 percent of your income as savings. It's a risk to go against the grain, to dare to think bigger than a 401(k). Every acquisition, every investment, every dollar spent is a risk. And it's precisely those risks that make us successful.

The important thing is that we don't take those risks blindly. We have to take our time and get thoughtful about what we're putting on the line. We have to identify what we're putting at stake and determine whether we're prepared to lose it. We have to prepare for the possibility that we might be wrong.

When we do that, our risks become something more than risks: they become *calculated* risks.

And you might say that calculating your risk is the key to mastering Stage Three. As circumspect and responsible as we aim to be, we always have to remember that this is the stage of the "Risk Taker"—it's the stage where we make the boldest plays in order to generate the biggest pay. For the first time in our lives, we are living by the maxim that *assets are greater than income*. We are daring to put income-yielding labor on the back burner so that we can prioritize *passive*-income-yielding acquisitions.

Risks and acquisitions are necessary. It's when those become the only things that define Stage Three that we're bound to take things too far. As the success goes to our heads, and as our egos take over, we'll overlook the possibility of failure. We'll only ever do optimistic modeling. We won't anticipate the possibility of a downturn or the possibility of injury or the possibility that we simply overlooked something. So we'll allow ourselves to become overleveraged. Vulnerable.

To make the most of Stage Three—and to evolve to Stage Four—we need to become strategic. Humble. We need to practice Pessimistic Modeling. We need to save carefully, live within our means, and make a point of never taking on debt that we can't afford to pay back.

In short, we need to *calculate* our risks. And we need to surround ourselves with people who can help us do just that.

———

FIND YOUR CONSIGLIERI

There is no better safeguard against risk than *people*. Relationships. Advisors you can trust. A good accountant will keep your income tax efficient while reliable risk managers and legal councilors will protect your finances from harm. Without these relationships in place, you are vulnerable. Exposed.

And yet, so many of us—even those of us who've made it to Stage Three—choose not to invest in these relationships. We might have professional advisors of some kind, but we don't take them seriously. We pay little for their services, and we don't consult them with any kind of frequency.

Very often, we aren't working with top-of-their-field professionals either. Our accountants are our poker buddies, or they're just the first accountants we ever met—the ones whom we've been with for fifteen years or more. We haven't considered the possibility that there might be better help out there.

For the most part, we make these mistakes for the same reason we make all of the other mistakes characteristic of Stage Three: our egos get in the way.

In the previous chapter and in the Introduction, we spoke about the three wealth-builder personality types: *Poor Me, Leave Me,* and *Transform Me.* In Stage Two, we saw the *Leave Me* mentality take on a defeatist quality: there, we adopted the belief that life couldn't possibly get better than retirement—that we would never be able to build fortunes greater than the sum of our savings. And we consequently refused to accept alternative philosophies of wealth.

In Stage Three, we discover a new kind of *Leave Me* mentality— one that isn't defeatist, but instead *overconfident*. As our asset holdings grow and our passive incomes swell, we become convinced that we've got it all figured out. So why, we ask, should we bother paying for expensive advice?

And so creeps in the second reason why Stage-Three thinkers often neglect their financial relationships: expense. Often, even while we're buying up assets and growing our passive incomes, we continue to fret over our savings. It's a vestigial anxiety that we carry over from Stage Two. We no longer have to worry about the possibility that we will run out of savings before we die, but we continue to cut corners and pinch pennies as though we might never earn again.

Ultimately, these anxieties about spending motivate us to adopt what I call a "GEICO Mentality" about our financial relationships.

Nowhere is this more prominent—or more baffling—than in medical and dental practices. Doctors will hunt far and wide for the most inexpensive insurance available to them. They'll report with pride that they saved $40 a month by switching to GEICO, neglecting to mention that the switch put tens of thousands of dollars at risk.

When it comes to insurance, you don't want the cheapest option. You want the most expensive one. You want the best one—the one that's going to cover you both from hell and from high water—the one that's going to support you and your family even in the event of catastrophic physical or financial setbacks.

Choosing the wrong insurance can prove to be a cataclysmic mistake. And that's the kind of mistake that good advisors can shield us from.

Whereas *Leave Me* personalities operate under the assumption that they're the smartest people in the room—that they don't need help of any kind—*Transform Me* personalities operate under the opposite assumption: they assume that there's always more to learn, that they're always going to have blind spots, and that the only way to grow is to surround themselves with the best and the brightest.

Instead of hunting far and wide for *good deals*, transformative personalities hunt far and wide for *quality guidance*. And they pay whatever it costs.

One of my clients, "Ted," is a megamillionaire who has no debt and the kind of life that most of us can only dream of. And that isn't thanks to me; he already had all of that when I first met him. Which is why, two days before that first meeting, he called me up to ask, "Why the hell am I meeting with you?"

He went on to point out that it was the middle of the day on a Wednesday, and he wasn't at work. He was calling me from his yacht. He said that he had millions in the bank and nothing to worry about.

"Plus," he added, "you're damned expensive."

I told him that his doubt made perfect sense, and that there'd be no hard feelings if he canceled. "Just drop my assistant an email," I said. "But if we don't hear from you, we'll assume you're coming."

Well, we didn't hear from him and two days later, when I got back from lunch, I found Ted sitting outside my office. I welcomed him in, and as he was sitting down, I said, "Ted, why the hell are you here?"

He asked me what I meant.

"You've got millions in the bank and nothing to worry about," I said. "Plus, I'm damned expensive."

Ted furrowed his eyebrows and thought for a moment before answering me. "Well," he said, "I figured you might tell me something I don't know."

Ultimately, I wasn't able to help Ted transform his finances. He already had all the money in the world. But I *was* able to help him transform his life. Together, we constructed a plan to make him happier, healthier, and wealthier. And by the time our first meeting was over, he was in tears. Whatever he was looking for, he found it that day in my office.

We'll spend some more time with Ted in chapter five. For now, my point is simply this: we can't grow—financially or otherwise—unless we believe that other people can help us, and unless we're willing to pay for that help. And if you talk to truly successful people—the sort of people who spend their Wednesday afternoons on yachts—you'll discover that those people are always looking to build new transformative relationships. They may be the smartest people in the room, but they'd always prefer to be the dumbest.

They'll also tell you that personal growth isn't the only reason to seek out top-notch advice. They'll tell you that it just makes good sense. When we pay for quality advice, we're paying a small portion of our present wealth to protect the entirety of our future wealth. We're ensuring (and insuring) our ability to purchase future assets, to grow our lifestyles, and to create impact.

As we'll see in chapter five, the waves that we make in Stage Three will have ripples that reach far beyond the visible horizon—and that's true for better and for worse. We saw how Chris's negligent investing hurt his son and his son's family. Likewise, later on, we'll see how smart investment strategies can benefit dozens, hundreds, and even millions of people.

This is why transformative wealth-makers—the sort of people who push past Stage Three, onto Stages Four and Five—prioritize their advising relationships no matter the expense.

Personally, when I find A-rated companies and specialists—people I can really trust—I throw money at them. Lots and lots of money. I do that because I know that they're probably going to save my butt someday. The odds that I will become disabled before age sixty-five are one in four.[15] And the odds that I will someday die are *four* in four. That's why I only ever hire advisors whom I can trust to protect me, my family, and my legacy no matter what.

Take your accountant for instance. Accountants are responsible both for identifying tax-efficient money-managing strategies and for preventing tax-reporting screwups. But if we favor inexpensive advice, and if we deny the possibility that the complexities of accounting may be over our heads, then we will likely end up bungling those strategies and diving headfirst into those screwups.

Working with business owners, practice owners, professionals, and consultants, there is not a month that goes by in which I do not see over $100,000 in accounting errors. Over the course of my career, I have seen tens of millions of dollars lost in overpaid taxes.

Perhaps worse are the unforced errors caused by the reckless and borderline-illegal tax-sheltering practices that ill-informed CPAs recommend to their clients. When entrepreneurs transform their legitimate businesses into tax shelters for personal expenditures, they expose themselves to audits. Ultimately, the cost of those audits far outweighs their tax savings. And it also far outweighs the cost of good advice.

Often, the problem here is not that our advisors are generally negligent. They might be very good at doing the work that they specialize in. The trouble is that they specialize in managing Stage-Two wealth. These are accountants and lawyers and risk managers who

---

15 "The Faces and Facts of Disabilities: Facts." *Social Security Administration. SSA. gov.* 2019.

specialize in helping people generate and protect savings in order to retire. And they're great at that work.

But when confronted with the financial and legal challenges of Stage Three, Stage Four, and Stage Five, these advisors find themselves in over their heads.

Relationships that were good for us in Stage Two become bad for us in Stage Three and beyond.

To journey beyond Stage Three, we need to learn that the cost of these bad financial relationships far outweighs the cost of good ones. And we need to embrace the reality that we can't always be the smartest people in the room. We need to stop settling for *good-enough* relationships. We need to stop risking everything in order to save nothing. We need to accept the basic truth that surrounding ourselves with our betters can only serve to benefit us.

That's why it's important that we use Stage Three as an opportunity to improve all of our relationships—not only our financial ones.

THE BEST AND THE BRIGHTEST

As we progress through Stage Three, it's not unusual to find that we begin outpacing and outperforming the people around us. Our neighbors and our friends are still struggling through Stages One and Two. They're wondering why their upward-trending incomes aren't making them any wealthier, or they're wondering why their downward-trending savings aren't making them feel any safer.

Meanwhile, we, the Stage-Three Risk Takers, are seeing everything go our way. We're acquiring assets left and right, and we're watching our passive incomes grow.

We've seen a few times now that the ego is like a parasite that feeds off our success. With every windfall, the parasite grows. And as it grows, it puts us more and more at risk, clouding our judgment and robbing us of the understanding that there's always more to learn.

This is why it's crucial that, as we grow, our friendships grow too. It's important that we surround ourselves with people who model the kind of lives we want to lead. Doing so will have the dual benefit of keeping us modest and revealing paths toward higher ground.

Personally, I can tell you that this past January, a client-friend and I made a handshake New Year's resolution that we would both devote this year to seeking out more friends who challenge us. Each of us wrote down a list of five people whom we would commit to meeting over the course of the next twelve months.

I made that commitment because I never want to be the biggest fish in my pond. Sure, being the biggest fish makes me feel nice about myself, but it slows my growth and puts me at risk of becoming over-confident. I want to sit in a room and know that I'm the smallest fish. I want to surround myself with teachers and guides and role models who can help me grow.

Organizational health specialist Patrick Lencioni has written about the importance of hiring team members who are *humble, hungry,* and *smart*.[16] And I think we should hold our friends to that same standard. If we do, they'll return the favor.

None of this is to say that you should ditch the people you care about or abandon the people who've stood by you through Stages One and Two. Of course not. In fact, in Stage Five, we'll see how important it is that you keep those people in your life and help them work toward achieving the same kind of wealth that you've achieved.

---

16   Lencioni, Patrick. *The Ideal Team Player: How to Recognize and Cultivate the Three Essential Virtues.* Hoboken, NJ: John Wiley & Sons, 2016.

All I'm saying is that balance is important: we should surround ourselves with people who remind us of where we come from, and we should also surround ourselves with people who remind us of where we're going.

They say that we are each the sum of the people that surround us—that you can predict your income by averaging out the income of your five closest friends.

That's what *they* say.

I'll simply say this: transformative people seek out transformative friends.

———

HUMBLE, HUNGRY, AND SMART

We just talked about surrounding ourselves with people who are hungry, humble, and smart. I said that we should hold our friends to that standard so that they'll do the same for us.

You might say that that's what this entire book has been about so far—staying hungry, getting humble, and becoming smart.

We begin our wealth journey as Dreamers—people who are full of hunger, but don't have the strategies in place to satisfy that hunger. Everything we earn, we consume. We save nothing. And that makes it impossible for us to build lasting wealth—to satisfy our hungers in the long term. Only by implementing the 70/30 principle—only by getting *smart* about our money—can we progress to Stage Two.

And then, at Stage Two, when we've finally become smart about saving our money, we lose our hunger. We stop dreaming and start fearing. We worry that we'll run out of money before we die. And so instead of pursuing extraordinary success, we settle for less: the prospect of a sedentary retirement. In order to unstick ourselves from Stage Two, we need to rediscover our *hunger*.

Now, in Stage Three, we finally begin to make serious movement toward wealth. We learn that assets are greater than income, and we acquire tirelessly. In the process, we grow colossal passive incomes, but we often lose perspective. Our successes go to our heads and our egos take over. Here, we need to dig deep and rediscover what it means to be *humble*.

At my firm, we work with lots of these Stage-Three Risk Takers. And I'll be honest with you: they're probably the most frustrating bunch of clients I have. Hubris is relentless—even more relentless than defeatism. It's hard to unstick Stage-Two Settlers from their determination to give up on life, but it's even harder to bring Stage-Three Risk Takers back down to earth—to help them rediscover their humility and their curiosity—to help them remember what it was like to learn from others and open themselves up to growth.

Perhaps what's most frustrating about working with Risk Takers is that they're *so close*. They're practically printing money. They have all the resources that they need. And all they have to do to propel themselves toward wealth is *take a breath*. All they have to do is get some perspective and acknowledge that they aren't always going to be the smartest people in the room.

In the most tragic cases, these Risk Takers never make it to Stage Four or beyond. They're just one bad month or one bad fall away from losing everything. They're overleveraged and doing nothing to protect themselves. You try to help them, but they just don't listen. And in the end, they pay for their pride. That's why it's so important to surround ourselves with first-rate advisors and practice Pessimistic Modeling.

Pessimistic Modeling prepares us for the worst. It reminds us what can go wrong and alerts us to our largest vulnerabilities in the process.

These models encourage us to live within our means, to pay off our debts, and to practice patience. Ultimately, by heeding these models' warnings, we can transform from reckless acquirers into strategic investors. We can collect tactical capital during market booms in order to maximize our purchasing opportunities when bubbles burst.

Meanwhile, practicing humility reminds us of both that we aren't always the smartest people in the room and that quality advice is priceless. Rather than penny pinch by doing it all ourselves—rather than save money by sticking with our Stage-Two advisors—we hunt for the top-flight CPAs, lawyers, and risk managers who are best equipped to protect us, our families, and our legacies. Likewise, we seek out friends who challenge us to grow—to never lose sight of our humility, our dreams, or the strategic thoughtfulness that will transform those dreams into realities.

Only by taking these steps can we truly enjoy the freedom that our new passive incomes offer us. Only by taking these steps can we proceed to Stage Four.

STAGE FOUR

4

THE
MANAGERS

FREEDOM. THAT'S HOW WE GOT HERE.

We wanted freedom.

When we began our wealth journey back in Stage One, we were motivated by dreams: dreams of time spent with family, dreams of traveling the world, dreams of nice cars, big houses, thriving businesses, and far-reaching foundations.

And then in Stage Two, we realized that we would never be able to realize those dreams on a fixed income. We discovered that a fixed income controls us—it restricts us. In order to realize our dreams, we were first going to have to achieve freedom.

Figuring that such a freedom would only be possible given a passive income stream, we spent Stage Three taking big risks, acquiring big assets, and earning big money.

And having done all of that, we're left to wonder: Are we any freer now than we were in Stage Two?

Very often, the answer is *no*. Very often, it's the people with the biggest income streams who are working the hardest. They're handcuffed to their businesses and to their assets. They're crushed under the certainty that if they were to step away from their work for even a moment, everything that they've built would collapse.

In short, you could say that as Stage-Three thinkers, we're money rich but time poor. And we have our egos to thank for that.

In the previous chapter, we saw that Stage-Three successes often overinflate our egos, and we explored how those overinflated egos can rob us of our money. But what we didn't explore are all the ways that our overinflated egos can also rob us of our *time*.

To believe that we are the smartest people in the room is to believe that we are the people best equipped to handle any given project. From signing clients to unjamming copy machines, there isn't any task that wouldn't be better off with our attention.

So we refuse to delegate. We micromanage. We overwork, we overcommit, and a month passes, and a year passes, and a decade passes, and we look up at our calendars to discover that we never took that trip around the world. We never spent that time with the family, never started that new venture. We never realized our dreams because we never realized that first, most fundamental dream of all: *freedom*.

Only in Stage Four do we discover that freedom isn't something that life affords us; it's something that we *create*. It's something that we choose.

> ## Once we do choose freedom, it's ours in an instant.

If we choose to go on micromanaging, overworking, and overcommitting, then we'll never generate enough bandwidth to live the life of our dreams. We have to *choose* to make time for ourselves. We have to *choose* to make time for our families and for our passions—for our ventures and for our *adv*entures.

And once we do choose freedom, it's ours in an instant. By the time we reach Stage Four, we've already got all the assets and all the passive income that we need. And we also have all the time that we need—it's been there all along. It's just been occupied. It's been waiting for us to free it up.

In Stage Four, our mission is to create freedom by evaluating and transforming the way that we spend our time. This stage is about discarding low-return burdens and delegating low-fulfillment tasks in order to free up time for those activities that we find most rewarding.

To put it simply, Stage Four is all about rethinking the way that we manage our time. And that's why I call Stage-Four thinkers "Managers."

ASKING THE MILLION-DOLLAR QUESTION

As Managers, our goal is to offload the tasks that bog us down in order to focus on the tasks that we find most rewarding. But that's a goal easier set than reached. When we're deciding which tasks to delegate and which to keep on our to-do lists, we often face some complex quandaries.

We might know that we want to spend less time traveling to pitch meetings, but we might also know that our pitches sign clients. We might not enjoy doing our housekeeping chores, but we also might not want to waste our money on hiring help. So we're going to need to figure out how to draw the line between practicality and extravagance.

If we're going to cut back on low-value activities and give ourselves the freedom to pursue our passions, we're going to need some sort of metric for determining what makes one activity worth our while and what makes another a waste of our time. We're going to need a framework for deciding when paying for help is prudent and when it's prodigal.

In order to make those determinations, there's a question that we're going to ask ourselves—and this is the question that's going to propel us through Stage Four, from start to finish. That question is: *What is my time worth?*

Asking and answering this question is doubly rewarding. First, as this chapter will demonstrate, answering this question gives us all the information that we need in order to start managing our time well.

And answering this question also helps us appreciate just how much we've grown since the beginning of our wealth journey.

Back in Stage One, we committed ourselves to the 70/30 principle, which stated that we ought to set 30 percent of our income aside as savings. When we did that, we earmarked one-third of those savings for personal development—books, classes, seminars, and workshops that would increase the value that we bring to our relationships, to our work, and to our lives.

For all this time that we've been implementing the 70/30 principle, we've been investing in our abilities, our acumen, and our awareness. And now we're reaping our reward. At Stage Four, we're going to concretely quantify just how much new value our personal development work has added to our time.

Having asked what our time is worth, we're going to calculate the answer in terms of dollars per hour. That figure is going to help us make smarter decisions about the way that we allocate our time, and it's ultimately going to become the tool that breaks our chains and frees us up to live the lives of our dreams.

In these next few pages, we're going to be taking an in-depth look at how that process works, both at home and at the office. But first, I think it's worth starting out here with a simple example of what I mean—one that will illustrate how calculating your hourly rate can radically transform the way that you spend your time.

BECOMING THE CEO OF YOUR LIFE

Imagine that you're traveling out of town for work. Let's say that you're based in Manhattan, and you've got a meeting to make in Boston.

Are you going to drive, or are you going to fly?

The drive to Boston is four hours. It's demanding, sure, but it isn't completely unreasonable. The downside of driving is that you'll kill four hours, and you'll probably end up feeling pretty worn out before your meeting. But the upside is that you won't have to buy a $200 plane ticket. And once you start thinking about return travel, the cost of flying doubles: $400 for a single meeting? How could that possibly be worthwhile?

Well, let's take a look at your hourly. If your time is worth $300 an hour, then the eight hours it takes to drive to Boston and back are going to cost you $2,400. By contrast, if you fly, you'll spend $400 on plane tickets, plus a combined total of three hours in the air, which means that you're looking at spending a grand total of $1,300 on this trip.

So not only will flying be more convenient, and not only will it help you preserve energy for your meeting, but it will also save you more than $1,000.

Suddenly the question isn't *how can you afford to fly*—the question is *how can you afford not to?*

And as you become better at managing your time, as you invest more in personal development, as your hourly rate rises, new questions will start to crop up. Questions like *Why are you driving yourself to the airport? Why aren't you paying for TSA precheck?* And, eventually, maybe someday even, *Why aren't you flying private?*

On the face of it, flying private can seem ludicrous. Instead of paying $300 for a flight, you pay $10,000. But what if your time is worth $10,000 an hour? Or $25,000 an hour? Even if you bill a fifth or a tenth of that rate, flying private could save you money. Between security lines, flight delays, boarding processes, and luggage carousels, commercial air travel can become an extraordinarily costly venture for someone who bills $2,000 an hour.

That's the kind of calculus that's going to govern this chapter—that's going to empower us to start living happier, healthier, wealthier lives.

We're going to start prioritizing efficiency over sticker prices. We're going to start discarding and delegating the low-return activities that hold us back—the activities that weigh us down, suck up our time, and monopolize our brain space. We're going to reduce the stress in our lives and increase the energy. We're going to start devoting our lives to the things that we love most.

> Honoring the value of our time actually makes our time even more valuable.

To make all of that possible, we're going to start treating time like it's our most valuable resource. We're never going to spend it on anything that doesn't yield either economic returns or personal fulfillment. In the final analysis, we'll see that honoring the value of our time actually makes our time even more valuable.

At the beginning of this book, I said that the principles of wealth development don't only apply to business owners—that they apply to all of us. And that remains true. But in this chapter, I'll propose that we can't become truly wealthy without first becoming CEOs.

Now, I'm not proposing that we have to become the CEOs of *Fortune* 500s, and I'm not even proposing that we have to become the CEOs of small businesses. I'm actually proposing that we have to become the CEOs of something much bigger and much more precious.

We have to become the CEOs of our lives.

Whether we're tech tycoons, or real estate moguls, or career technicians, we're going to have to begin managing our time, our resources, and our relationships with focused intention. We're going to have to begin staffing up and staffing out, surrounding ourselves with a network of deeply passionate, highly competent employees and advisors.

Learning to do this will transform our lives. For the first time, our assets won't control us. The economy won't control us. For the first time, *we* will be in control. Which means that for the first time, we will be really and truly free.

THE FOUR BOXES THAT WILL CHANGE YOUR LIFE

So far, we've seen that the first step toward becoming successful Managers is calculating the value of our time. Now, we're going to take the next two steps: we're going to put together a list of the activities that currently occupy our time, and we're going to determine which of those activities actually deliver a value that matches our hourly rate.

So let's start with the first of those two new steps: let's put together a list of activities that currently occupy our time.

To be clear, I'm not speaking figuratively here. I'm recommending that you sit down and list every single activity that you perform in a day, a week, a month, a year. And as you might recall from the list making that we did in chapter two, I'm going to insist that this list *be thorough*.

As with any large project, you're going to want to break this list-making process down into smaller, component pieces. Start by splitting your activities up into two categories: the activities that you perform in your work life and the activities that you perform in your personal life.

When it comes to listing out the tasks that we perform in our work lives, it's important to include out-of-office activities as well. By Stage Four, most—if not all—of our income is coming from our assets. And all assets have to be managed. Properties need to be maintained. Portfolios need to be monitored. Every one of those individual tasks needs to be on our list.

Once we've finished listing our work activities, we'll start listing out all of our personal activities. How do we spend time outside of the workplace and outside of the marketplace? This includes everything from mowing the lawn to sorting the mail to cooking dinner for the family.

If it takes up time, it goes on the list.

Once we've finished making our lists, we'll be ready for the second part of this process—the part where we determine which activities actually deliver a value commensurate with our hourly rate.

While some of our activities will have clear dollar values—like an attorney's document review, which gets billed hourly—many of our activities don't. It's difficult to put a dollar value on a sales call, and it's even more difficult to put a dollar value on teaching your daughter to hit a ball, to cook a cannoli, to code in Python.

So instead of trying and failing to quantify the value of these activities, we're going to abstract the notion of value into two key categories of benefit: economic return and personal fulfillment.

You'll need a pencil and paper for this.

Are you ready?

We're going to start by drawing a simple two-by-two grid . We're going to label the x-axis *Economic Return*, assigning one column the value *Low* and the other column the value *High*. Then, we're going to label the y-axis *Personal Fulfillment*, likewise defining one row as *Low* and the other as *High*.

ECONOMIC RETURN VS PERSONAL FULFILLMENT

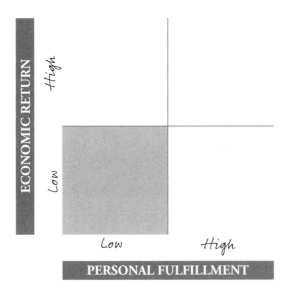

I'm sure you can see where I'm going with this. The *Economic Return* columns are going to help us distinguish between those tasks that yield little cash and those that yield lots of cash.

Meanwhile, the high and low fulfillment rows will measure how much we enjoy what we're doing. How much energy does it give us? How much passion do we have for it? How grateful are we for the moments spent on those tasks? Do we love doing these things? Would we do them for free?

When we compare this grid to our list, we should be able to assign economic return and personal fulfillment values to each item.

For instance, we might label *Mowing the Lawn* as a low-return/low-fulfillment activity while labeling *Training Team Members* as a high-return/high-fulfillment activity .

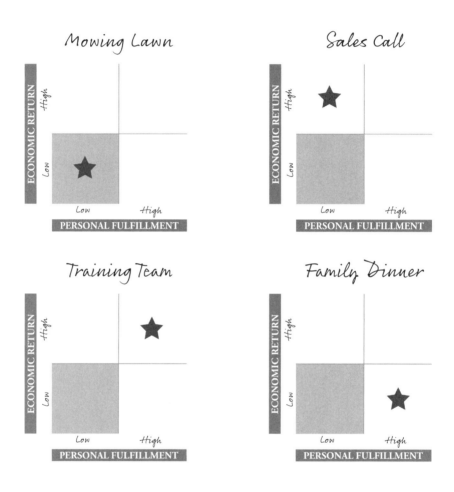

Again, I'll ask you to recall those two rules that governed our list making back in Stage Two. *Be thorough* was the first, and we've already seen how that comes into play at this stage. And now that we're ascribing value to the activities that fill our time, it's important to remember the second rule: *be honest.*

For some of us, key aspects of our jobs might not offer us much fulfillment, while mindless household tasks might reward us with much-needed meditative downtime. That's fine.

Nobody's going to look over your shoulder. Nobody's going to judge your list. If we want to build happier, healthier, wealthier lives, it's crucial that we become honest with ourselves about what we do and don't value. Only then will we be able to make the most of our time. Only then will we be able to reduce the time that we spend on low-impact activities—the activities that don't earn us money, that don't make us happy, that don't generate energy, inspire passion, or deepen our relationships with the people around us.

Only then will we be able to eliminate mundane tasks. Finally we'll be able to start focusing on the activities that we enjoy and the people whom we love.

THE 70/30 PRINCIPLE OF TIME MANAGEMENT

Back in chapter one, I suggested that in order to achieve wealth, we have to learn how to handle our money, and I introduced a 70/30 principle of cash management that would help us do just that. Now we're discovering that in order to achieve wealth, we must also learn how to handle our time, and so I'm going to be introducing a 70/30 principle of *time* management.

It's a simple one, really. All it says is this: 70 percent of your time should be devoted to activities that you find highly fulfilling.

But beware: while the 70/30 principle of time management is a lot more fun than the 70/30 principle of money management, it isn't much easier to execute. Pulling back from low-fulfillment tasks and responsibilities can often be quite a difficult process.

But I swear to you—it's going to pay off. And not in some sort of subtle, long-term way either. If the quality of our lives is measured by the moments that we spend doing what we love, then the 70/30 principle of time management essentially just *makes us happy*. Its sole function is to compel us to fill our lives with moments spent living.

Looking back at our two-by-two grid, we'll recall that there are two categories of activities that offer high degrees of personal fulfillment: those that yield low economic returns and those that yield high economic returns.

ECONOMIC RETURN VS PERSONAL FULFILLMENT

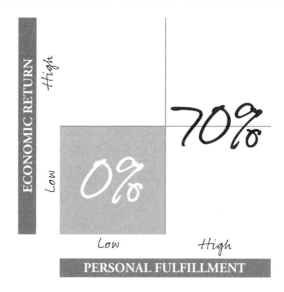

The activities that offer both high personal fulfillment and high economic returns are the ones that both make us money and make us happy. These are the workplace activities that we enjoy most. Sometimes they're the ones that made us choose our career paths in the first place, and sometimes they're the unanticipated passions that we discovered as we grew into our professional roles. Whatever their origin, these activities thrill us—they keep us curious about and engaged with our work, and they reward us with high financial payouts.

No less important are those activities that offer high personal fulfillment despite the fact that they yield low economic returns.

Some of these activities will be things like hobbies and pastimes, which we love despite the fact that they don't make us any money. I suppose that, technically, you could argue that these activities have economic value insofar as they give us the downtime that we need in order to come back to our work refreshed, recharged, and ready to go. But, really, I think it's a mistake to write off hobbies and pastimes as means to an end.

Hobbies and pastimes are essential components of well-lived lives. Sailors and painters and Sunday-afternoon mechanics aren't just looking for restfulness in their hobbies. They're looking for the beauties and the marvels of life that aren't visible from the windows of their fiftieth-floor corner offices.

And then, of course, there's the low-return/high-fulfillment time that we devote to *each other*—to our friends, to our children, to our spouses. No matter how high our hourly rates rise, they will never overshadow the value of time spent in relationship.

Before I built my firm, Tower Leadership, I worked at an asset management firm where standard hours were nine to five. I liked to get in at seven—brew some coffee, power up my computer, and get a head start on the day. Every morning I'd go in hoping to have the office to myself for a few hours, and every morning I'd be disappointed. There was always one guy who'd beat me to the office.

We'll call him Greg.

By seven in the morning, Greg would be typing away, with his jacket off, his tie loosened, his sleeves rolled up, and a pair of takeaway coffee cups at his elbow.

Looking back, I'd say that there were two big differences between the ways that Greg and I approached our work.

The first was our hours. Greg would get in before me and leave after me. I was always out of the office by five o'clock. I wanted to be sure that I could be home in time for family dinner, in time to catch up with the kids, help them with their homework, tuck them in, read them a personal finance book, and kiss them goodnight.

But while I was helping my son memorize his times tables, Greg was still at work. He'd stay until midnight, one, two, or three in the morning.

Greg was nothing if not devoted. But the strange thing was that his extra hours didn't pay off. And that was the second major difference between the ways that Greg and I approached our work: I was successful and Greg wasn't. My client retention rate doubled his, and my clients' satisfaction surveys scored me twice as high.

For all the extra time that Greg was putting into his work, he wasn't actually extracting any more value. He was working two times harder and yielding two times less. And that's because the activities that brought him to the office early and kept him there late weren't high-yield activities. They were activities that I'd chosen to delegate.

By devoting his time to these low-yield activities, Greg was tiring himself out and stretching himself thin. As a result, he'd end up mismanaging that tasks that actually mattered. He might have invented the perfect filing system, but his client-facing deliverables were always riddled with errors.

Meanwhile, because I was delegating and because I was recharging at home, I was able to devote more energy to higher-yield tasks. I ascribed a great deal of value *to* my time, so I was able to extract a great deal of value *from* my time. Meanwhile, Greg didn't value his time, and for that reason, he wasn't able to create any value with that time.

And who suffered as a result?

Everyone.

Greg. Greg's clients. And most of all, Greg's family.

Every entrepreneur someday encounters the reality that building a business costs time. Every specialist knows that training costs time. Every professional someday faces off with a gargantuan, potentially career-altering project that demands everything of them.

There will be phases of your life when the best thing that you can do for yourself and your family and your business is pull an all-nighter, spend a weekend at the office, or cancel a vacation.

But those moments are few and far between.

They're faint, anomalous blips on the vast timelines of our lives.

In the long run, if we prioritize our assets over our lives, everything will suffer: our clients, our finances, our families, and ourselves.

I can't emphasize this enough: no matter how high our hourlies climb, they will never outsize the value of our family lives and personal lives. Your time might be valuable, but your *quality* time is *in*valuable. It's crucial to understand that low-return/high-fulfillment activities can be the most important activities of all.

But that realization raises an interesting question: what about the opposite activities? What about high-return/low-fulfillment activities? What about those activities that make us lots of money, but don't give us any joy?

WHEN A HIGH RETURN ISN'T HIGH ENOUGH

Twenty years ago, my client Clare decided to enroll in dental school. She found the process of operating on teeth fascinating. She couldn't imagine that it would ever get old. Eventually she completed dental school, trained at her discipline, developed a stellar reputation, and opened up her own practice.

Designing implants and building bridges stayed interesting for a long time—for a decade or more. But eventually, a new fascination started to emerge: as Clare built and grew her practice, she found herself becoming more engaged with her entrepreneurial work and less engaged with her dental work.

She already knew how to fill cavities, crown teeth, and extract dying nerves. What she didn't know was how to generate leads, how to sign patients, how to grow a team, and how to franchise out. As the business of business became more and more rewarding, the business of dentistry became less and less fulfilling.

Meanwhile, she found that she could make an exponentially greater impact on her community by stepping out of the operatory. If she spent her days drilling and filling, she could only see a dozen or so patients in a day. But if instead she spent her days training and managing a team of five younger doctors, she could impact sixty patients in a day. If she opened a second office, she could double that figure. And by giving more attention to marketing strategies, she was able to grow local awareness about the importance of maintaining dental health.

For Clare, the activities surrounding business ownership had become high-fulfillment tasks, while the activities surrounding direct dental care had become low-fulfillment tasks. The trouble was that those low-fulfillment dental-care tasks were still yielding high economic returns : placing implants and dental bridges brought lots of money into the practice.

Eventually, Clare came to me asking where these high-return/low-fulfillment activities fell with respect to the 70/30 principle of time management. Should she be trying to offload these tasks or should she be giving them as much of her time as possible?

"Clare," I said, "didn't you just tell me that by training five doctors, you could reach five times as many patients?"

"Yeah," she said.

"So then," I asked her, "doesn't mean that you could be producing five times as much?"

It was absolutely true that if Clare personally operated on patients, she could bring a lot of money into the practice. But that didn't mean that having Clare operate on patients was a high-return strategy.

You see, high return and low return are relative terms. As a dental surgeon, Clare could bring $5,000 into her practice a day. But as a business owner and team manager, she could bring in $25,000 a day. Given those figures, dental procedures were actually *low*-return/low-fulfillment tasks.

It takes most dentists and physicians years to learn this lesson, but once they do, it transforms their practices: *You can make more money out of the chair than in the chair.*

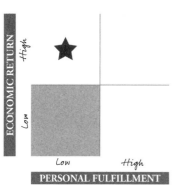

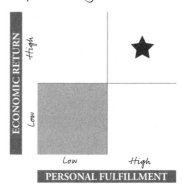

And this principle isn't only true for dentists and physicians. It's true for all of us. Low-fulfillment activities almost never yield high returns in *relative* terms. We can almost always get higher returns by focusing on the tasks that we love. Which means that really, the box for high-return/low-fulfillment activities ought to be eliminated altogether.

If a task isn't *emotionally* rewarding, then it isn't rewarding at all. Stick it in the box for low-return/low-fulfillment activities and delegate it.

ROOT, ROOT, ROOT FOR THE HOME TEAM

Now it's time to start delegating these low-return/low-fulfillment tasks.

These activities don't excite us. They don't invigorate us. And they don't make us any richer. All they do is weigh us down and hold us back, monopolizing time that we could otherwise spend earning well and living well. So we're going to get rid of them.

Back at the beginning of this chapter, we said that Stage Four would be devoted to creating freedom. Well, this is how we create freedom.

We're going to break these low-fulfillment tasks down into three categories, and we're going to delegate them to three different kinds of support teams. By the time we're finished, we're going to find that our lives are happier, healthier, and wealthier. And we're also going to find ourselves surrounded by networks of highly skilled professionals who are committed to supporting our growth.

Let's begin at home, with the *domestic* activities that hold us back—the chores that keep our home lives in order but give us no joy.

Now, as I said earlier, it's important not to discount the value of pleasurable housekeeping tasks. Some of us cherish the time that we spend mowing the lawn, cleaning the dishes, doing the laundry, washing the car. Maybe we find these tasks meditative or maybe we just get a kick out of them, plain and simple.

But we need to *really* get a kick out of these activities in order for them to represent good uses of our time. If you're billing clients $2,000 an hour, then the hour that you spend mowing the lawn is *costing* you $2,000.

You have to ask yourself: Does lawn mowing give you $2,000 worth of personal fulfillment?

If the answer is yes, that's terrific! Enjoy your life!

But for most of us, the answer will be *no*.

The vast majority of our housekeeping tasks don't fulfill us in fundamental ways. And they yield exactly no economic return. The time that we spend cutting grass, drying silverware, hanging clothes, and scrubbing the windshield is time that we could otherwise spend generating leads, making sales, and developing products. It's time that we could be spending catching up with our friends, connecting with our children, and bonding with our spouses.

In order to offload these low-fulfillment tasks, we need to assemble what I call a *home team*—a team of professionals who specialize in helping busy business owners, technicians, consultants, dentists, and doctors free up their time. These teams often include specialists like housekeepers, gardeners, and—if you're as bad a cook as I am—perhaps a chef.

Although Stage-Two thinkers often consider hiring a home team to be an extravagant, unreasonable expense, Stage-Four thinkers recognize that by paying $30 or $40 an hour, they can save thousands of dollars' worth of time. And because home teams specialize in domestic work, they're often freeing up not just our time, but our *quality* time, which is worth a great deal more than thousands of dollars. Quality time is priceless.

I can tell you that one of the best decisions I ever made was the decision to hire someone to do my laundry. It sounds so simple: all Gina does is wash my clothes, dry my clothes, and hang them up in my closet. But in the process, she saves me an extraordinary sum of time and mental energy.

After I hired her, my Sundays suddenly became completely free: I could focus on being with my family. I could take the kids swimming. I could take them to a baseball game, to a museum, to a library. I could help them with their homework instead of folding their laundry.

And, at the personal level, my wardrobe no longer occupies any of my brain space. Every morning, I walk into my closet and find everything I need laid out—folded, hung up, color coded. As if it's been there all along, just waiting for me.

The small hourly fee that I pay for these affordances is trivial compared to the value that I get back in terms of time and mental energy.

This is what it means to become the CEO of our own lives. Just as CEOs of businesses hire accountants, lawyers, and marketers to manage their corporate affairs, we, as CEOs of our lives, assemble home teams to manage our domestic affairs.

So why don't more people hire home teams?

Well, there's the extravagance objection, which we've already debunked. And then there's another objection. It's one that—I should warn you—I find a bit repugnant.

When I introduce clients to the notion of hiring a home team, there are quite a few who tell me that, in the case of their particular family, a home team isn't necessary. They say that they don't need to hire help.

"So you're going to spend three billable hours a week doing laundry?" I'll ask.

"No," they'll say. "My spouse does that."

And that just pisses me off.

Most of the time, there are vile, backward gender politics at play here. And even when there aren't, this remains a downright *crappy* attitude—one that signals to me that these clients aren't ready for Stage Four—that they're still trapped in Stage-Three thinking.

As the previous chapter illustrated, Stage Three is often dominated by egotism. When I'm at Stage Three, everything is all about me all of the time. And now, when we pass the buck of household chores on to our spouses, our egotism is growing at the expense of our loved ones.

Within this mental framework, it doesn't matter if my spouse is hassled or unhappy. It doesn't matter if their time is wasted. As long as I'm freed up for fun.

In addition to being selfish, this attitude is also shortsighted. If your spouse is hassled and unhappy, then that's the energy that's going to define your marriage. You're going to find yourself in a relationship governed by resentment and dissatisfaction. Whereas, if your spouse is energized and engaged, then your marriage is going to likewise become energizing and engaging. Your relationship is going to be defined not by temper and exhaustion but by passion and enthusiasm.

To these clients, I say: *just imagine.* Imagine what your spouse could achieve if freed of the obligation to perform low-return/low-fulfillment housework. Imagine the energy that they could bring to their own professional ventures, to charity work, to artistic expression, to parenting, to your marriage.

When we marry, we form a partnership. That partnership can be parasitic or it can be symbiotic. It can be exploitative or it can be supportive. If we want our partnership to become symbiotic—if we want it to become supportive, then hiring a home team is one of the most powerful moves that we can make. Doing so will foster mutual success, mutual growth, and mutual happiness.

YOUR PERSONAL BOARD OF ADVISORS

So that's the first category of low-yield work that we can unload from our lives: *domestic* work. It's perhaps the easiest category for us to identify as checking off both the low-fulfillment and low-return boxes. There aren't many people out there who get a kick out of scrubbing pots and pans, and there's *nobody* out there who gets paid to do it—not when it's their own pots and pans that they're scrubbing.

But not all low-return/low-fulfillment tasks are going to be so easy to identify. In fact, there's an entire category of low-return—or even *negative*-return—activities that most of us mistakenly believe will yield high returns: these are *strategic* activities.

Here, I'm talking about tasks like drawing up contracts, completing taxes, and choosing insurance providers. Those of us who aren't lawyers, CPAs, or risk management specialists tend not to derive deep personal satisfaction out of performing these sorts of strategic tasks. But we take these tasks on anyway—at least portions of them—because we believe that doing so will yield high returns.

In the most extreme cases, that could look like drawing up our own contracts and doing our own taxes. More often, it looks like hiring low-fee, low-insight advisors—the sorts of advisors we won't be able to trust. When we hire these advisors, we condemn ourselves to performing hours of research, verifying the accuracy of our advisors' guidance.

In these cases, we tend to think that taking on these tasks will yield high returns insofar as we'll be saving money. But the reality is that these tasks don't save us any money at all. In the best cases, they cost us billable hours; and in the worst cases, we end up executing misguided strategies to cataclysmic effect. We end up with a bad contract, a bogus tax return, a useless insurance plan, and suddenly we're facing a lawsuit, or an audit, or the bankruptcy of our business.

Now we're not just looking at a low yield—we're looking at a *negative* yield.

This may sound like a rehash of what we discussed back in chapter three, but my experience has been that it's not until Stage Four that wealth builders start taking the value of good guidance seriously. And that's because Stage Four gives us a new perspective on the cost of bad advice.

In Stage Two, our goal was to pay advisors as little as possible. We were saving to retire, and we couldn't afford to pay a penny more than was absolutely necessary. Every time we paid a fee, we worried that we were putting our retirement in jeopardy—we worried that we were increasing the likelihood that our money would run out before we died. Then, in Stage Three, we began to appreciate the financial consequences of bad strategies, so we started upgrading our advising relationships.

The trouble is that, in my experience, this Stage-Three upgrade of advising relationships tends not to be so easy. To the Risk Taker, that upgrade doesn't feel wise. It feels like a gamble. We're spending money on advice today because we're betting that it will save us money tomorrow.

At Stage Three, our attitude toward money has evolved, but we retain the vestigial anxiety that every invoice we receive might have the power to ruin us. Paying big fees to top-notch advisors terrifies us. We only do it because we're persuaded that bad strategies will lose us even more money down the road.

Only when we reach Stage Four do we discover that losing money shouldn't be our primary concern. We discover that losing *time* should be our primary concern. Once we're billing at $5,000 or $10,000 or $20,000 an hour, the idea of doing our own research to double-check our advisors' guidance becomes absurd. The idea of inviting a tax audit by hiring a bargain-priced CPA becomes preposterous.

At Stage Four, we're very happy to pay somebody $1,000 an hour in exchange for top-tier, sure-thing, incontrovertible advice because that advice isn't just saving us money; it's saving us time. And time is the most valuable resource of all.

This is why, in addition to assembling a home team, Stage-Four Managers also assemble what I call *a personal board of advisors*. As we become the CEOs of our own lives, it's crucial that we recruit lawyers, accountants, and risk managers whom we can trust to steer us right.

But hiring a team to assist me in my capacity as the CEO of my life is one thing. Hiring a team to assist me in my capacity as the CEO of an actual business is something else entirely. And that's what we'll look at next.

ROOT, ROOT, ROOT FOR THE BUSINESS TEAM

Now we're down to our third and final category of low-return/low-fulfillment activities: our *business* activities. In the workplace, the distance between time well-spent and time poorly spent is often vast and easy to eyeball. It's clear as can be that some tasks are going to grow my business, give me energy, and inspire me with passion, while others are simply going to suck up my time—either because they're inherently low-return tasks or because I'm just not very good at them.

For me, managing my calendar is the quintessential example. I hate doing it. And historically, it's gotten me into some pretty big trouble.

To be clear, managing a calendar doesn't have to be a low-return activity. This whole chapter is devoted to the idea that smart scheduling grows wealth. I'm just saying that when *I* manage a calendar, the return is worse than low. It's negative.

I once called up my assistant to put a client dinner on the calendar.

"Just double-checking that I heard you right," she said. "Did you just ask me whether you have anything on the evening of March 17?"

"Yeah," I said. "Why? Do I already have something scheduled?"

"Yeah," she said. "Your son's birthday."

I don't know what it is. There's just something about seven-day weeks, four-week months, and twelve-month years that breaks my brain.

But guess what: there are people out there who *love* managing calendars. There are people who have *very strong opinions* about the best ways to color-code conference calls and the most efficient strategies for syncing schedules. Talking about calendar-keeping makes them downright *giddy.*

I don't understand it. I don't relate to it. But I know it's true.

So I found one of those people, and I hired them.

And because I now have someone managing my calendar, I'm able to devote more of my attention to the tasks that I'm good at—the tasks that matter to me—that grow my firm, make me money, and give me joy.

This is how we delegate low-yield workplace activities. We build powerful, unified business teams. We take those tasks that we aren't competent at, that absorb our time, that drain our energy, that leave us feeling unhappy or unfulfilled, and we hand them over to team members who *love those tasks.*

In addition to freeing you up to focus on money-making, passion-inspiring, joy-generating tasks, a strong team will also help you transform your company into a self-managing enterprise.

In order to facilitate the seamless handover of these tasks, you'll find yourself creating the roles and building the systems necessary to scale your business. And as you stack your team with strong leaders and brilliant specialists, you'll discover that the company runs just fine without you. For the first time, you'll find the freedom to step away without remorse and without anxiety—with the confidence that your business continues thriving even when you're out of the office.

None of this is to suggest that you absolutely must own your own business in order to reach Stage Four of your wealth journey. If you look at successful executives, directors, and technicians, you'll see that they're utilizing exactly the same principles at the department and project levels. Instead of micromanaging teams or hoarding new initiatives to themselves, they're doing everything they can to bring their direct reports into the fold. They're training and coaching younger team members, and they're delegating without hesitation.

Whether you own a business or you're employed by one, your strategy should be the same: you want to surround yourself with highly competent, highly passionate people who can help carry the load. By delegating the tasks that don't inspire or enrich you, you'll free up time to focus on the ones that do.

As with rest of Stage Four, all of this only becomes possible once you begin defining and honoring your hourly rate. That rate is going to help you determine which tasks do and don't deserve your attention.

Once you start implementing this strategy, you'll find that enforcing your hourly is like alchemy. The more you value your time, the more valuable it becomes. It's basic supply and demand: as you become better at managing your time, the demand for that time will go up while your willingness to supply it will go down. As a consequence, the cost of your time will rise. It will become more valuable.

This is why, at Stage Four, we no longer worry about paying big fees to advisors or high salaries to employees. Nor do we fret over time spent away from work. As Managers, we understand that these things don't actually cost us money. They *make* us money. And, more importantly, they give us freedom—freedom to connect with our families, grow our communities, and pursue our dreams.

And that's the philosophy that will ultimately transport us to the fifth and final stage of wealth development: the philosophy that we actually create our wealth by spending our wealth.

———

WHAT'S NEXT?

In order to really understand this idea of giving more to get more, we need to take a step back and look at how we got to Stage Four—how we managed to create freedom.

We didn't start pursuing freedom in Stage Four. This project dates back to Stage Two, when we saw retirement as the key to liberating ourselves from our work and creating time for the things that matter most to us.

So, if we've been pursuing freedom since Stage Two, why has it taken us so long to catch up with it? Why does our Stage-Four strategy succeed where our Stage-Two strategy failed?

Well, let's look at how those strategies differ.

In Stage Two, our plan was to stop working and stop earning at age sixty-five. Once retirement began, we would simply live off our savings, which meant that our assets were going to go down over time. Every day, we'd have a little bit less left in the bank. And that was just fine with us, so long as we could be sure that we'd die before our money ran out.

At Stage Two, choosing to follow our passions meant choosing to spend money. Which meant choosing to *lose* money. And because we weren't going to work anymore, we expected that we would never be able to earn that money back.

This is all to say that, from the standpoint of Stage Two, freedom was an *expense*.

But in Stage Four, freedom becomes an *asset*. As Managers, we free up our time in order to spend it on tasks that yield us high returns. Namely, *spending time makes us money*.

In part, this Stage-Four evolution is made possible by the assets and the passive income that we acquired during Stage Three. At Stage Two, we might not have been able to afford the home teams, the business teams, and the boards of advisors that are now freeing up our time.

> What we have here is an evolution from a scarcity mindset to an abundance mindset.

But the evolution that we've undergone is bigger than that. It's about more than money. It's about philosophy.

At Stage Two, we believed that time *cost* us money. But in Stage Four, we understand that time actually *makes* us money. The more we manage it, the more valuable it becomes.

So what we have here is an evolution from a scarcity mindset to an abundance mindset.

Stage Two was defined by a scarcity mindset. Our lives were governed by the belief that there would never be enough—never enough money and never enough time. Every bill we paid, every task we performed, every day we lived cost us money. Hiring a home team, a business team, and a board of advisors would have meant reducing the size of our savings. And that was untenable.

It's not until Stage Four that we begin adopting a true abundance mindset. Now, for the first time, instead of conceptualizing the world as a place of scarcity, we conceptualize it as a place of plenty. Every hour that we spend working *brings us more*. Every task that we perform *brings us more*.

Now it isn't scary to hire a home team. It isn't scary to hire a professional team. It isn't scary to pay big bucks for a board of advisors that we can trust. Because each of these expenditures guarantees that we will earn more—that we will get more out of our lives.

You might say that at Stage Four, we finally rediscover the idealism of Stage One: we remember that anything is possible—that our capacity to achieve is infinite.

It's at Stage Four that we truly begin to transform our lives. We become intentional about the way that we spend our time, devoting it to the activities that we find most rewarding. And as we learn to value our own time, we learn to value the time of others too. It isn't long before we find ourselves surrounded by a community of family, friends, advisors, and teammates who, like us, are making the most of their lives—living happily, energetically, productively, and with passion.

We create this Stage-Four life by adopting an abundance mindset—by approaching our work and our lives with the philosophy that there will always be more.

It's worth noting that this abundance mindset will never be accessible to people who approach wealth-building with *Poor Me* or *Leave Me* attitudes. The abundance mindset is fundamentally transformative and so it requires a *Transform Me* attitude.

The abundance mindset is defined by the belief that everything we give to the world will bring more back to us. That belief is a direct byproduct of the *Transform Me* principle that life always has more to offer: there's always more to earn, always more to learn, always more to achieve.

As I'm sure you can tell, I love Stage Four. The Managers are some of my favorite people to work with. There's just one little problem with them—one little problem with Stage Four and the abundance mindset and the *Transform Me* approach to wealth-building. And it's a problem that ultimately makes it very difficult for Stage-Four Managers to *remain* Stage-Four Managers.

The problem is that people who have abundance mindsets and *Transform Me* personalities are always looking for opportunities to grow and to do more.

Once they've built their home teams, once they've built their business teams, once they've surrounded themselves with top-tier advisors—once they've organized their lives in such a way that every minute is devoted to high-reward activities, they're left with a skin-tingling, brain-bending, mind-maddening question that makes it impossible for them remain at Stage Four.

And here's the question:

What's next?

STAGE FIVE

5

THE
HUMANITARIANS

JESSICA AND I WERE IN OUR TWENTIES,

newly married and headed south for Christmas. Our destination: Grandpa Gus's.

Jessica's grandfather lived in Tampa, Florida. We were scheduled to be there at 5:00 p.m. sharp to sing carols, eat dinner, and exchange gifts with Jessica's family. We figured that if we left at 8:00 a.m., we could stop for lunch, and make it with time to spare.

It was a straight shot down the I-75, so I locked in the cruise control and queued up the music.

Hours passed. We stopped. We got some lunch. And then it was back in the car, back on the I-75, back on cruise control, and back on the radio.

We couldn't have been more than thirty minutes from Grandpa Gus's when we hit it.

Not a truck. Not a car. Not an animal. But a puddle.

We hit a puddle.

And our world turned upside down.

Literally.

Or at least I think it did.

I don't remember much about the car accident, but I remember that we hydroplaned—badly. Fortunately, all of the car's safety features did what they were supposed to do, and Jessica and I walked away without a scratch.

But the same could not be said of our Chevy.

One look at the shattered glass and accordioned plastic told us everything we needed to know: the only trip our car had left in it was a trip to the junkyard.

One sixty-dollar cab ride later, Jessica and I were sitting in Grandpa Gus's living room apologizing for having arrived so late—and without any gifts. We'd left a dozen books, toys, and Apple products strewn across four lanes of highway.

Of course, Jessica's family told us not to worry. All anyone wanted to do was inquire about our health and feed us cold turkey.

While Jessica fended off a second serving of some suspicious-smelling stuffing, Grandpa Gus grabbed me by the shoulder.

"Come with me," he said.

With that, he steered me out of the living room, down the hall, and into his study. He sat me down in a leather armchair, and then perched himself on the edge of his mahogany desk.

Grandpa Gus was the sort of man who seemed to get taller every year he was alive. He might have been white haired, limping, and as old as time, but even then, his mind was sharper than mine will ever be.

"So, Eric, let me ask you. You have insurance?"

I told him we did.

"How much do you think you'll get for the car?"

"Five grand," I said.

"That's not a lot of money."

I agreed with him.

"You're gonna buy another car?"

I figured we'd have to.

"You think you'll find one for five grand?"

"Probably not."

"So what're you gonna do?"

"Take out a loan, I suppose."

Gus shook his head. "Taking out a loan doesn't sound very smart to me."

I didn't know what to say to that.

"You know, I've got a brand-new Lexus in the garage."

I didn't know what to say to that either.

"But what I really want is a *golf cart*."

With that, Gus reached into his pocket, drew something out, and tossed it at me.

"I figure $5,000 would buy a pretty good golf cart. Don't you think, Eric?"

I looked in my lap and saw what he'd thrown. It was a Lexus key fob.

"How's about we make a trade?" he said.

Grandpa Gus had grown up hard, in a sod-floor home. He lost his mother at the age of two. As a boy, he knew that he'd need a craft to call his own, so he went to the library, borrowed a book on carpentry, and put himself to work. Eventually, he taught himself to build barns. He taught himself to build a business. He taught himself how to invest, how to grow his money, and eventually, how to live the life of his dreams.

By the time I knew him, he'd been on boards of banks, been around the world, accumulated all the money he needed to live the life he wanted. He had done all the things he ever wanted to do. There wasn't anything left that he wanted for himself.

But for his *family*?

For his family, he wanted everything.

When I asked Gus why on earth he'd hand over his brand-new Lexus in exchange for $5,000, he gave me the simplest answer in the world.

"Because you married my granddaughter."

———

Stage Four seems like it should be the final stage of wealth development. You've got plenty of money coming in. You've got plenty of money in the bank. You've got high-yield assets generating powerful passive income streams. And you're making the most of your time—you're giving it to your family and your friends and the projects that inspire you most.

Our journey toward wealth began with our dreams, and now we have all the money and all the time that we need in order to realize those dreams. So we're finished, right?

Well, if you had a *Leave Me* mentality, then the answer to that question would be an unequivocal *yes*. You'd say that you've got it all figured out, and that there's nothing left to do—nothing left to learn.

The trouble is that if you had a *Leave Me* mentality, you wouldn't make it to Stage Four in the first place. You can only get to Stage Four if you have a *Transform Me* mentality. And if you've got one of those, then you won't accept the notion that Stage Four is the final stage of wealth development.

As *Transform Me* personalities, we believe that there is *always* more to learn—always more to achieve. And so, after we get to Stage Four, and after we *master* Stage Four, we don't want to stop. We look around and ask, "What's next?"

Well, I'll tell you what's next: we have to change our mentalities. The next thing that we have to do is change the fundamental nature of ourselves. And that means that it's time to stop saying *Transform Me*.

Once we've mastered Stage Four, the *Transform Me* mentality can no longer serve us. As big and abundant and powerful as that mentality is, there is also a problem with it—a big, *big* problem with it. And that problem is the last thing left that's holding us back.

That problem is the word "Me."

Transform *Me*.

By the end of Stage Four, that just isn't enough anymore. I've got money coming in. I've got money *piled up*. I've got all the assets and all the time in the world. *Me* is taken care of. It's time to take my inward gaze and send it outward.

It's time to Transform *the World*.

When we reach Stage Five, we're more than Dreamers, more than Settlers, more than Risk Takers, and more than Managers. At Stage Five, we become *Humanitarians*.

For the Humanitarian, impact is greater than assets. Impact is greater than income. Impact is greater than anything else.

For the Stage-One or Two or Three or even Stage-Four thinker, swapping out a $60,000 Lexus for a $5,000 golf cart doesn't make any kind of sense. Any way you slice it, you're down $55,000.

But Stage-Five thinkers understand that money isn't an end in itself. Money is just a tool that you use to fill your life with purpose. And $55,000 is a small price to pay for purpose.

In Stages One through Four, we try to fill our lives with purpose by transforming ourselves. But it's never enough. In Stage Five, we realize that to truly fill our lives with purpose, we have to look beyond ourselves. We have to transform the world around us.

For some people, like Gus, that means transforming the lives of family members. For others of us, it's about transforming the lives of friends. For me, my cause is the fight against child cancer. For other people, it's the fight against global warming, against hunger, against AIDS. For some, it's about promoting their political ideals; for others it's about supporting the arts. Some people build businesses to transform the world. Others build foundations or trusts. What they all have in common is the Humanitarian belief that creating impact is the key to fulfillment.

The irony is that when Humanitarians give their money away, they don't get any poorer. They actually get wealthier.

And I don't just mean that figuratively.

As we proceed through this chapter, we'll discover that the fastest route to wealth is the one that we chart through charity. To change the world, Humanitarians need to earn more, save more, build more, and create more.

> You will earn more dollars if you give more dollars.

So they end up becoming, quite simply, *richer*.

It doesn't sound true. It doesn't sound possible. But I promise you that it is both true and possible.

You will earn more dollars if you give more dollars.

To begin, all you have to do is ask:

WHOSE LIFE DO YOU WANT TO CHANGE?

As a former navy man, I'm always hearing stories about vets and about wisdom gained at sea. One of my all-time favorites is the story of a navy pilot by the name of Captain Charlie Plumb. During the Vietnam War, Captain Plumb flew F-4 Phantoms on seventy-four successful missions. On the seventy-fifth, he was shot down, captured, tortured, and imprisoned. Plumb lived out his life as a prisoner of war in an eight-by-eight cell for 2,103 days before being released.

Years after he returned home, Plumb found himself at a restaurant, shaking hands with a stranger.

"You're Captain Plumb," the stranger says.

"That's right," Plumb says.

"You were part of that TOP GUN outfit," the stranger says.

"That's right," Plumb says.

"You were shot down off the aircraft carrier *Kitty Hawk*. You parachuted into enemy hands, and you spent six years as a prisoner of war."

Plumb just looks at this guy, lost. "How in the world did you know all that?" Plumb asks.

And the stranger smiles. "I'm the guy who packed your parachute."[17]

For Plumb, that guy has become a metaphor for all of the people in our lives who support us—all the people who pack our parachutes. And for me, it's become the first and most important answer to the Humanitarian's most pressing question.

Even the richest people in the world must confront the incontrovertible reality that nobody can help everybody. Even kings and queens and sultans, even Gates and Buffett and Bezos can't afford to help *everyone*.

So, as a Humanitarian, you have to make a choice. You have to ask: *Whose life am I going to change?*

My answer: the person who packed your parachute.

Who made an impact on you? Who helped you get where you are today? Who saw your potential, who taught you, who coached you, who supported you through thick and thin? Who made it possible for you to achieve all that you've achieved?

It might be a parent, or a teacher, or an assistant, or a friend. Or it might be a complete stranger—a fresh recruit packing parachutes below deck.

Whoever they are, they've changed your life. And now you have a responsibility to change theirs.

---

17 "Captain Charlie Plumb." *Charlieplumb.com.*

Often, we exploit—or, at least, underestimate—these parachute packers during the early stages of wealth development. For instance, as Stage-One, Stage-Two, Stage-Three, and Stage-Four business owners, we worry about whether our teams are overpaid, or whether we're spending too much on employee benefits. But at Stage Five, we realize that none of that matters. What matters is helping the people who are helping us. What matters is the impact that we make on the people around us.

Making a smart financial decision is important. But at Stage Five, we realize that it's not *more* important than making an impact. At Stage Five, *nothing's* more important than making an impact.

Impact always yields more than assets.

That's what Grandpa Gus meant when he said that giving Jessica and me his brand-new Lexus was a no-brainer. If there was a way that he could impact his family, he was going to take it.

In the previous chapter, we saw that quality time always yields more than work time. Well, a similar principle applies here: *impact always yields more than assets.*

So look around, figure out who packed your parachute in the past, who's packing it now, and do what you can to help them. Only after you've done that can you—in good faith and good conscience—turn your attention to other people and other causes.

Now, it's important to acknowledge that while parachute packers are the *first* answer to the question of whom you ought to impact, they're not the *only* answer to that question. Once you've got your parachute packers taken care of, and you're ready for your next cause, this dilemma comes up again: *Whose life are you going to change next?*

And from here on out, I don't believe there are right answers. I'm sure there are people out there who have strong feelings about whether it's more important to fund the arts or to revitalize the environment—people who believe that one disease needs to be cured before another, that one cause matters more than the next—who think that leaving money to your church is somehow better than leaving money to your children.

But I think that's all nonsense.

Philanthropy is not a math equation. There isn't a right answer. There's a whole world of people and causes out there, and the only way to decide which ones to help is to *follow your heart*—whether that means endowing a scholarship, dedicating a building, supporting a loved one, or building a foundation.

THE MORE YOU GIVE, THE MORE YOU GET

When we're in Stage One and Two and Three, the idea of prioritizing impact over assets—the idea of actively *looking* for opportunities to give away money—sounds downright bananas.

Actually, it sounds worse than bananas.

It sounds *terrifying*.

Sure, we agree that, theoretically, it would be nice to do some charity work. But won't that charity work ruin us financially? If we give it all away, won't we lose everything? Won't we lose our shot at comfortable lifestyles, at stability, at our dreams? Will we have to give up our houses and our cars and our boats? What about our time with our loved ones? Will we have to trade all of that away for the opportunity to make an impact?

> ## We can either be givers, or we can be takers. There's no in between.

The short answer is no.

And the long answer is also no.

Ultimately, giving away our money will actually make us *more* money.

There are very few things in this life that are black and white. But here's one of them: we can either be givers, or we can be takers. There's no in between.

There's just no away around the fact that if we aren't focused on *giving* to the people in our lives, we're going to end up *taking* from them.

We might not *mean* to take from them. We might not do it with duplicity or with malice. In fact, we could be really, really nice about it—be the kindest, warmest, most pleasant takers in the known universe. But if we aren't actively giving, then we will end up taking. If our attention is only on ourselves and our own wants and needs, then we will end up benefitting from the efforts of others—at the *expense* of others.

And even if we were to put ethics and morality and categorical imperatives aside for a moment, we would see that this kind of taking-oriented mentality will hit our own wallets harder than it will hit anyone else's. Because the way that people relate to us directly affects what we earn. And people don't relate well to takers: at worst, takers seem like adversaries, and at best, they're simply uninspiring.

By contrast, when you establish yourself as a giver, you establish that your goal is to make a difference in other people's lives. And that *does* inspire people.

As a giver, you won't only be giving away your *stuff*—you'll also be giving away your *philosophy*. You won't only be sharing your *money*—

you'll also be sharing your *vision*. Which means that people are going to learn what you know and what you believe, and they're going to want to get involved. They'll want seats on your board. They'll want desks in your office. They'll want to be in your rolodex of friends, clients, mentors, and collaborators. They'll want to advise you, fund you, work for you. They'll want to be a part of accomplishing whatever you've set out to accomplish.

And the people you attract will be givers themselves. They'll be the sorts of people who want to fight for you, for your mission, for your organization. They'll be inspired to show up at night, show up on weekends, and give whatever they can to your cause—whether it be time, labor, guidance, or cash.

As a giver, you attract more people, you attract more resources, and you attract more money.

Imagine that you own a business, and the purpose of that business is to make you wealthy. Not because you're callous or evil—just because you have dreams and need money to realize them.

Well, if your goal is to enrich *yourself*, then you're going to try to get as much work out of your team as possible, for as little pay as possible. Not because you're some kind of villain—just because that's how our economy works.

Meanwhile, your team—or "employees" in this case—are going to recognize that this business is designed with only one purpose in mind: to make *you* wealthy. So they're going to wonder what's in it for them. Talented people will leave your organization and all you'll have left will be the takers—people who are only going to look after themselves. They're going to slack off. They're going to miss some things, ignore others, and half ass the rest. Some might even become actively insubordinate. And, eventually, they're going to quit.

Ultimately, your company is going to suffer, and so is your wallet.

But if you built a business with a mission—a business meant to *transform the world*—if you built a business with the intention of supporting and growing the members of your team, then you'd get entirely different results.

In this kind of business, you wouldn't treat your team members like commodities. You'd treat them like family. You'd try to make an impact on their lives—try to mentor them and give them opportunities to grow. Instead of negotiating salaries down, you'd make an active effort to give your team the best salaries and the best benefits they've ever received. And meanwhile, these team members would see that their work is about more than quarterly earnings—that it's about changing the world for the better.

Wouldn't these team members want to help you? Wouldn't they want to see your company succeed? Wouldn't they want to give this work their all? Wouldn't they stay longer, grow faster, and take on more responsibility? In the process, wouldn't they make your business more scalable? Wouldn't they make it more successful? Wouldn't you see bigger returns? Wouldn't you see more income? Wouldn't you and your team and the world around you be better for it?

The answer, of course, is *yes*. Yes, yes, yes—yes, yes—yes, yes, and yes.

Meanwhile, I've found that once my clients begin prioritizing impact, their strategic planning also grows infinitely better—which makes it possible for them to climb up the ladder of wealth faster while simultaneously growing and strengthening their safety nets. As Humanitarians, our contracts become clearer, our insurance policies become safer, and our incomes become more tax efficient.

In earlier stages, our strategies were only really designed to protect *us*: *our* finances, *our* companies. Which meant that we were effectively accountable to no one. If we screwed up, the only people who'd suffer were ourselves.

But now, in Stage Five, we're accountable to the world around us. Our strategic planning isn't meant to protect us alone—it's meant to protect our legacies. It's meant to protect our families, our friends, our communities, our organizations, our causes.

The stakes are growing, so our strategies have to grow too. And, as a consequence, our finances end up being better protected—our resources better allocated.

Master salesman Zig Ziglar is often quoted as having said, "You will get all you want in life if you help enough other people get what they want."[18] And I couldn't agree more.

In the early stages of wealth development, we create income and assets and time in order to help *ourselves*. In Stage Five, we create income and assets and time in order to help *others*. And the irony is that when we prioritize other people, everything that we send out into the world comes back to us tenfold. The more you give, the faster you earn. The more you care, the more you'll be cared for.

So if you're worried about whether you'll ever have financial stability, whether you'll ever be able to live that life of luxury, whether you'll ever be able to realize those dreams, then the best thing that you can do for yourself is *give it all away.*

I know that sounds contradictory, but it's true. You have to create impact in order to create success.

---

18   Primary source not found. Often attributed to Zig Ziglar. See "Zig Ziglar: 10 Quotes That Can Change Your Life." Forbes.com. November 28, 2012.

X = YOUR LEGACY SQUARED

Now, while some of us may worry that giving away our money will hurt our finances, others of us initially get into Stage Five precisely *because* this Humanitarian business sounds like such a great racket: we figure that we'll prioritize impact, make lots of money, and look great doing it.

And I actually think that's fine.

It doesn't matter *why* we start focusing on impact. The important thing is *that* we start focusing on impact. Because once we do, we will inevitably discover that creating impact creates meaning. We'll discover that even while we're enjoying our newfound riches—our nice cars and our big houses—we're enjoying our Humanitarian work even more—that it's delivering an unparalleled degree of pride and satisfaction.

We'll find that getting out of bed is easier and more exciting every day. We'll feel motivated to work harder than we ever have before, to earn more, to build more, because we'll see the impact that our work and our cash and our organizations are having on the world around us.

In short, we'll discover how much more rewarding life is when we're *Transforming the World*.

When I use that phrase—*Transform the World*—I think it might sound like hyperbole—like perhaps it's meant to be a metaphor. But it isn't hyperbole. And it isn't a metaphor. Stage-Five thinkers actually can *Transform the World*.

Back in Stage One, we talked about the Compound Effect. We said that if you invest time, money, and energy into personal development, those investments will compound to yield extraordinary returns—a better bank statement and a better life.

Well, when you invest in impact, those investments also compound—they compound to create what I call the "Ripple Effect."

Let's flash back to the fifties for a moment—a time when a generation of WWII veterans was struggling to find its role in a changing country. One of those patriots was a man named Earl Schoaff, whose heart condition had prevented him from serving in the military. Undeterred, Schoaff had joined the American Field Service as a medical volunteer, and had done additional damage to his heart in the process.

Now, after the war, he was struggling to find his peacetime, stateside identity. He was living with his parents and pressing suits for a department store. Then, one day, as legend has it, Schoaff's next-door neighbor took him to a lecture being given by a man called Dr. J. B. Jones.

The lecture was about the nature of success, and it was a barn burner. Inspired by what he heard, Schoaff connected with Jones, who eventually agreed to take the young man under his wing. For years, Schoaff trained with Jones and eventually became a prominent public speaker in his own right.[19]

Meanwhile, another department store clerk, Jim Rohn, was struggling to create a better life for his family when a friend invited him to a lecture. This time, the lecturer was *Schoaff*, and the cycle repeated itself.

Rohn loved the speech and got in touch with Schoaff. Schoaff took Rohn under his wing, and Rohn eventually became one of the most prolific motivational speakers of his generation.[20]

---

19   This site has no verifiable references, but also seems to be the only source for biographical information on Schoaff; it's also the sole source for Schoaff's Wikipedia entry: "About John Earl Schoaff." EarlSchoaff.com.

20   Again, I was only able to find one source on Rohn's biography, and it has no references: Givens, Mark. *Jim Rohn: Biography and Lessons Learned from Jim Rohn Books...* Self-published, Amazon.com.

Decades later, a janitor found himself in a hotel ballroom, listening to Jim Rohn speak. That janitor's name was Tony Robbins, and today, he is the most prolific motivational speaker of *his* generation.[21]

Now Tony is spearheading what he calls the "One Billion Meals Challenge"—a campaign that, at time of writing, has delivered almost five hundred million meals to two hundred food banks across the country.

Tony's aiming to fund a billion meals by 2025.

A *billion* meals. All because J. B. Jones devoted his life to making an impact. He took the time to make an impact on Earl Schoaff, who took the time to make an impact on Jim Rohn, who took the time to an impact on Tony Robbins.

And that's how the Ripple Effect works.

Almost a hundred years ago, Dr. J. B. Jones shook Earl Schoaff's hand. Since then, that handshake has had a century of reverberations. And by 2025, that handshake will have yielded a billion meals.

You absolutely *can* transform the world. You might not know how it's going to happen, and you might not *see* it happen. But if you devote yourself to a life of giving, then it *will* happen.

And when I talk about giving to transform the world, I'm not just talking about writing a check. The transformation that you create won't just be a product of the *money* you give. It will also be a product of the *philosophy* that you pass on to others.

Look at Earl Schoaff, at Jim Rohn, at Tony Robbins. None of them were given wealth by their mentors. They were given *wisdom*. They then leveraged that wisdom to *create* wealth. And eventually, to create *change*.

---

21   Robbins, Tony. *MONEY: Master the Game.* New York: Simon & Schuster, 2014, Chapter 3.4.

You might even say that your philosophy is the single greatest asset that you can give away. I know that in my own experience, the wisdom that Grandpa Gus gave me has proven to be exponentially more valuable than the car that he gave me.

And I *loved* that car.

Wealthy people do all sorts of incredible, generous things to establish legacies. They dedicate buildings, endow scholarships, give to charities. But those aren't the only things that you can do to create a legacy.

You aren't limited to giving away money. You can also give away your *philosophy*.

You aren't limited to creating a legacy of giving. You can also create a legacy of *impact*.

And when you do, you don't just double the magnitude of your legacy—you don't just 4x or 10x or 20x your legacy. You *square* your legacy. You multiply your legacy by an order of magnitude equal to *itself*. You create a Ripple Effect that can literally *Transform the World*.

IT'S A BITTERSWEET EPIPHANY

Back in Stage Three, we encountered a client of mine whom I called "Ted." When I first met Ted, he was already a megamillionaire. He had everything he could ever want—the cars, the boats, and all the time in the world.

And so, at first, he was skeptical about whether meeting me would really be worth his time. He figured that he was already living the life of his dreams. What more could I help him achieve?

The Wednesday before we met, he called me from his yacht and put that question to me directly. He asked me point blank: "Why the hell am I meeting with you?"

I didn't have the answer, and I didn't pretend to. "I don't know," I said.

The only thing I *did* know—which I didn't tell him—was that there *was* a reason.

Ted was right: on paper, his life was perfect. But the very fact that he'd gone to the trouble of scheduling a meeting with me meant that *something* was missing.

Later that week, Ted showed up at my office. He handed over his financials. He told me about his earning history and his expectations for future growth—everything that he was planning to do in order to get richer before he died. And then he asked me whether there was anything that I'd do differently.

And I told him.

I told him what I believe.

That impact is greater than assets.

That wealth isn't created by earning.

That wealth is created by giving.

I showed him how he could use his resources to dedicate a building, found a charitable trust, and bring his children into his philanthropic work.

I showed him how he could pass a philosophy of impact on to his son and on to his daughter.

I showed him how he could change the lives of literally *thousands* of people—how he could create a legacy of impact that would propel his work forward for generations to come.

I showed him how he could use his resources to *Transform the World*.

What Ted realized over the course of that day was that he'd

spent his whole life chasing financial success without ever stopping to ask *why*.

As we got to talking, I discovered that he had the potential to become the ultimate poster boy for the five stages of wealth development. First, as a Stage-One thinker, he'd chased income, and he'd found that his income kept disappearing on him: the more he earned, the more he spent. So then he moved to Stage Two and started chasing savings. But it felt like he could never save enough. So then he broke the mold and decided to do what none of his peers were doing: chase assets. But the more he managed to earn, the harder he had to work. Even after he got more control over his time in Stage Four, he still felt like something was missing.

Deep down, Ted knew why he'd scheduled that meeting with me: he'd scheduled that meeting because his life was incomplete—because something was missing. And on the day we met, he realized what it was.

The thing that was missing was a *reason*.

A lifetime of white-knuckling his way through traffic. A lifetime of long hours and big paychecks, of victories and sacrifices, of profits and cuts and deals and sales and liquidations and terminations and in all that time, he had never stopped to ask the most important question of all.

Why am I doing this?

And now, all at once, and for the first time, he was asking that question and discovering his answer: *I did all of this so that I could transform the world.*

It's for days like this one that I keep a box of tissues in my office.

Ted came into my office skeptical and rudderless, and he left feeling more optimistic than he had in decades.

He left with a *purpose*.

None of this has anything to do with *me*. I didn't perform some kind of financial magic. Ted didn't learn some kind of brilliant new tax trick from me. All I did was prompt Ted to investigate what might be possible—what he could achieve with the time that he has left in this world. And the power of that possibility moved him to tears.

Lots of tears.

I let him keep the tissue box.

The next time I met Ted, he said that he was feeling more excited and more optimistic—warmer and younger—better than he'd felt in years. But he said that he was also feeling more than a little bit bitter.

He was bitter about all the years he'd wasted on frivolous expenditures when he could have been creating impact. He was bitter about all the opportunities he'd missed for financial and personal growth. He was bitter about all the people he hadn't been able to help. And he was bitter about the financial advising industry that had led him astray.

Ted had worked with dozens of advisors over the years, and none of them had ever brought up the notion of impact. All they'd ever spoken about was what they could double and what they could triple—what Ted could buy, could invest, could yield. Because the only thing that Ted's advisors had ever really worried about was their cut.

And Ted's just one example.

I've had similar experiences with countless clients. They'll come to me for help: they want to double their money, they want to franchise their firms, they want to get revenues up to $100 million. And they have no idea why.

Then we sit down. We talk it through. We explore what wealth really means. And time and time again, I find that my clients are moved to tears—are *overjoyed*—when they discover just how much impact they can create. They become inspired and thrilled in a way that no purchase, no acquisition, no car, no house, no yacht has ever inspired or thrilled them. They become downright *devoted* to transforming the world around them.

And then they realize one day, with a shock, that they could have been creating impact along.

They realize how unfortunate it is—maybe even how *sick* it is— that we aren't educated to think about impact. That we're educated to think only about ourselves. *My* income. *My* retirement. *My* house. *My* car. *My* boat. My *everything*.

We're educated to focus on those things even though those things can't help us. They might make us rich. But they won't make us as rich as we could be. And they certainly won't make us wealthy. They won't make us really and truly happy.

We're never educated to ask *why*.

We're never educated to seek true fulfillment.

> The only path to *true wealth* is the one we take by giving.

If we were, then the world would look like a very different place.

The moment you ask why, you know the answer: the only path to fulfillment is the one we chart through impact. The only path to *true wealth* is the one we take by giving.

That's the discovery that we make in Stage Five: that wealth and fulfillment are the same thing—that they're reached the same way.

Once people reach Stage Five, they realize that if they'd focused on impact from the beginning, they could have earned more, built more, achieved more, and given more. They realize that everything would have been easier, and that the world would be better for it.

That's why the number-one question that I get from Stage-Five thinkers is often a rhetorical one:

Why haven't I been thinking about impact all along?

START WITH THE END IN MIND

At Stage Five, we make another related discovery: that Stage Five does not exist. We discover that just as the language around the *Transform Me* mentality was broken, so, too, the language around *Stages of Wealth* is broken.

There are no *stages*. There are no *levels* you have to pass through. There are only *philosophies*.

A philosophy that my income can transform me.

A philosophy that my savings can transform me.

A philosophy that my assets can transform me.

A philosophy that my personal time can transform me.

And a philosophy that my generosity can transform *the world*.

Once we understand that these are not stages but instead philosophies, we realize that we don't have to pass through one philosophy to get to the next. We can skip straight to adopting the philosophy that's most rewarding.

We realize that there's no connection between what we currently earn and what we can achieve. We realize that we can build anything, and that we can give everything.

Once we understand that wealth is a philosophy, we begin to appreciate that we don't need personal fortunes to achieve wealth.

That's what makes people like Ted so frustrated with the education system and the finance industry. When people like Ted become Humanitarians and start living full, fulfilled lives, they realize that they could have been living that way all along. They didn't have to wait to be sixty, sixty-five, seventy years old, rich, and successful. They could have been Humanitarians from the beginning. They could have been giving generously from the beginning.

They could have started with the end in mind.

Don't believe me? Think we need to have lots of money to make an impact? Think we need to be Bill Gateses and Warren Buffetts before we can start to give back?

Well then, consider the case of immigrants.

Consider the people who leave everything behind—the comfort of their homes, their families, their friends, their communities, their native languages—in order to create better lives for the generations that will follow them. Consider the people who put everything on the line in order to transform their families' futures. Consider the people who cast themselves into lions' dens of racism and xenophobia, who work three jobs, who deny themselves every comfort in order give their grandchildren—whom they might never meet—a shot at living better lives.

As far as I'm concerned, that's Humanitarian thinking at its finest.

And it's a kind of thinking that pays off.

We all know immigrants and descendants of immigrants who've risen to the tops of their industries and achieved extraordinary wealth. If you think about it, the overwhelming majority of wealthy people in the United States fit that profile. After all, nearly all of us are descendants of immigrants. And even if we are struggling, nearly all of us are better off than our ancestors.

My point is that you can *start with the end in mind.* You don't need riches to start making an impact. You just need the right philosophy.

In fact, my experience has taught me that getting rich doesn't make it even a little bit easier or a little bit more likely that a person will start giving back. I've found that if people aren't willing to give away ten cents on the dollar, then they won't be willing to give away ten million dollars out of a hundred million dollars.

But while getting rich won't make it any easier to create an impact, creating an impact *will* make it easier to get rich. Much, much easier.

Business coach Dan Sullivan often talks about the idea that it's easier to grow your company by a factor of ten than it is to grow your company by a factor of two.[22] And while that might sound counter-intuitive at first, it makes sense when you think about it.

If you're trying to scale up by a factor of two, then you're going to create a strategy for small, incremental growth. But if you're trying to scale up by a factor of ten, then you're going to have to create a strategy for extraordinary, *rapid* growth. You're going to have to acquire a different collection of skills, a different set of resources, a different community of collaborators.

To 10x your organization, you're going to need to learn how to attract the help of extraordinary people. And you *will* attract the help of those people. Because extraordinary people are attracted to extraordinary challenges. Hungry, humble, smart people don't want to take baby steps. They want to take giant leaps.

When you build an organization with *10x* in mind, you'll see incredible results.

And when you build an organization with *impact* in mind, you'll see the same results *squared.*

When people realize what you're trying to achieve—the kind of positive change that you're trying to affect in the world—they're going to want to help. Badly. They might even *pay* to help.

After all, that's how nonprofits work.

I'm working with a woman right now, "Victoria," who has a business that she's trying to grow. Not so that she can live larger, but so that she can give bigger. Her goal is to someday build a $35 million charitable trust.

---

22   Sullivan, Dan. "Episode 38: Dan Sullivan Shares Why Growing 10x is Easier than Growing 2x." 10xTalk.com. September 10, 2014.

In part, Victoria's doing this for her family. But she doesn't want to leave this money behind for her children to *gamble* away. She wants to leave this money behind for her children to *give* away. She wants to give her kids the opportunity to live philanthropic lives. She wants to help them help the world transform.

And while Victoria's financial targets sound extraordinarily ambitious, I don't have a doubt in my mind that she'll reach them.

For one thing, I know that she is incredibly dedicated to her work—precisely because she's so dedicated to her goal. If she were just trying to put away money for her next Mercedes, I think she'd burn out. But every crisis she faces, every deal she closes, every call, every email, every single task she performs gets her closer to her goal of transforming the world. So she gives every one of those tasks her all.

And her mission also attracts people who want to help her—people who are inspired by her vision and want to be a part of realizing it. People like me.

As much as I try to give all of myself to every single client, there's no denying the fact that I work harder for *this* client. Because I believe in what she's trying to achieve.

Will I take weekend calls for work? Absolutely not.

But will I take weekend calls for Victoria? Absolutely.

And will I charge her for every call? Of course not.

Because I want to transform the world. And Victoria is helping me do just that.

So I absolutely believe that she's going to reach her $35 million goal. If she had no job and a thousand bucks to her name, I'd *still* believe that she's going to reach her goal. Because achieving wealth doesn't require oodles and oodles of money. All it requires is the right philosophy.

As Humanitarians, we discover that wealth isn't linear. It's circular. It's a feedback loop. You don't start poor, accumulate lots of money, and then achieve wealth. Instead, you give to others, and you receive wealth back. You give away what you've received, and you get *even more* back. You give and you get. You give more and you get more. On and on, until, like an avalanche, your cycle of wealth gains so much mass and so much momentum that it permanently transforms the landscape.

It transforms you.

It transforms the world.

As Humanitarians, we discover that impact doesn't have to be the final stage of the wealth journey.

It can be the first stage.

The end is really the beginning.

CONCLUSION

FOR ME, THIS ALL BEGAN WITH A BOAT.

I was working at a mainstream asset management firm years ago, and I'd given a great deal of my attention to one client in particular—we'll call him *Raphael*.

Raphael was a tough nut to crack. It had taken me the better part of two years to gain his trust. But gain his trust I had.

The moment you met Raphael, you could tell that he came from old money. He wore Gucci loafers, waxed nostalgic about life on Long Island, and generally carried himself like the world was his—and had been since birth.

The first day I met him, he walked into my office, slammed his briefcase on my desk, and said, "You've got thirty minutes to prove that you're worth my time. Otherwise I'm leaving, and I won't be back."

Then he sat down, leaned back, and set a timer on his watch.

I was certainly put off by his entrance, but I was not deterred. We got to work, and when that timer went off, Raphael didn't leave. He paid for an extra hour.

And a week later, he came back and paid for a few more.

You see, Raphael had the kind of paycheck where you've got to count the zeros twice to be sure. But he also had debt. Lots and lots and lots of debt. And he needed my help to get rid of it.

As far as I was concerned, Raphael was a dream client. Sure, he was a jerk—no question. But he had extraordinary financial potential. We met a few times and put together a strategy for cutting spending, growing income, and paying off loans. Then, we executed on that strategy.

And it worked.

Within twenty-four months, we had all of Raphael's debts paid off. We'd reached every single financial goal that we'd set for ourselves.

To celebrate, Raphael and his wife, Page, invited me to dinner. We toasted to a future full of savings and growth, we congratulated each other on a strategy well conceived and well realized, and then, sometime between the soups and the salads, Raphael, whose face was flushed red with wine, leaned over and said, "There's just one catch."

I laughed preemptively at whatever joke he was queueing up. "What's that?" I asked.

"I bought a boat," he said.

And I laughed again.

And then, I tilted my head and thought for a moment.

It had the construction of a joke, but it wasn't actually funny.

"What do you mean?" I asked.

He looked at Page and he laughed and she laughed and he said, "I mean I bought a boat."

"Like a motorboat?" I asked.

"Like a yacht," Page chimed in.

"You bought a *yacht?*"

He laughed again. "It just got delivered yesterday."

Then he pulled out his phone and showed me his lock screen.

Where a picture of his kids should be, there's a picture of the *Gale*.

That's the name of his yacht.

"How much did this thing cost?" I ask.

"About six mil," he says.

And that was that.

The end of my relationship with that client.

The end of my relationship with that firm.

The end of my relationship with whatever the hell "asset management" is supposed to be.

I didn't tell Raphael and Page right then and there. I finished the dinner to be polite. But I took care of the check and fired them a few days later. And I quit that job not long afterward.

Raphael and I had worked so hard to create a new life and a new paradigm for him and for his family—one free of debt, free of stress, and free of constraints—one in which it would be possible to realize dreams and create impact—create *meaning*.

And he'd thrown it all away. For a boat.

To be clear, I didn't have any moral or philosophical issue with him buying a boat. I think people should do whatever it takes to bring joy into their lives. Whether that means buying a Ferrari or buying a mansion or buying a yacht named *Gale*. I believe that people should have the opportunity to experience everything that life has to offer, and that includes flights on private jets and weekends spent at sea.

But I also believe that there's *more* to life. I believe that we can set the bar higher. I believe that we can pursue something that's a heck of a lot bigger than lifestyle luxuries, and I believe that if we do, we'll get all those lifestyle luxuries along the way.

What I came to understand for the first time that night—as I quietly sipped my soup, and as Raphael and Page pitched each other on increasingly absurd maritime destinations—was that *owning a boat* had been Raphael's primary goal from the start. Over the course of the last two years, we'd spoken about things like scale and liquidity, but those had simply been code words. Euphemisms. They'd simply been adult, roundabout ways of talking about Raphael's childish obsession with buying toys.

I didn't want to enable that kind of behavior anymore.

And that *is* what I had been doing. I'd been enabling Raphael and hundreds of other clients like him. That's what the finance industry is *designed* to do.

Financial advisors are in the business of selling investment products. That's it. And the way they do that is by perpetuating philosophies of wealth that prioritize savings and acquisitions—the hoarding of *money* and the hoarding of *things*.

> I made a promise to myself that I would build the rest of my career around that one question: Why?

And, that night, at dinner, I realized that I had been doing precisely the same thing for my entire career. I had encouraged my clients to accumulate. I had enabled my clients to acquire. And I never, ever asked *why*.

If I *had* asked why, then I would have found out that the answer was *boats*. But I didn't. I didn't ask because it wasn't my job to ask.

But it is now.

Now, I *make* it my job.

After that night, I made a promise to myself that I would build the rest of my career around that one question: *Why?*

It's a question that I put to myself, to my team, and to my clients every single day.

From everything I've done, and everything I've heard, and everything I've seen, I've come to believe that the best answer to the question *Why* is *Impact*. So, with that end in mind, I built a firm that would focus on training and empowering leaders—people who would be committed to creating impacts of their own. In that way, I figured that I could create a ripple effect and do my part to transform the world.

Sure, revenues are important to our business. And sure, we have earning goals. But for us, the thing that gets our team members out of bed in the morning is *impact*. It's the heartfelt emails and the tearful hugs—it's the thanks we get and the stories we hear about people who've turned their financial lives around and, in doing so, have turned their *entire* lives around—people who've been able to transform themselves and transform the world around them because we helped them find the resources to do it.

For nearly all of us, our journeys toward wealth begin with a broken philosophy—one that we've been taught since we were children. And that's the philosophy that achieving wealth is all about earning more—driving up income and driving up revenues until we're as rich as Rockefellers.

Ultimately, though, that philosophy fails us because focusing on incomes distracts us from focusing on outcomes. We watch what we earn but not what we keep, and so we never get any richer.

So we change our strategy. We begin fixating on accumulation and stability. Our families, our financial advisors, and even our governments persuade us that retirement is the ultimate form of wealth. Buying into that common wisdom, we accumulate compulsively while always fearing for the worst: What if the market crashes, what if our money's stolen, what if we inadvertently outlive our savings?

We escape that "Settler" paradigm only when we begin to *build*: we build up our assets, we build up our knowledge bases, we build up our networks. We acquire relentlessly in order to generate a third kind of wealth—one that's defined by the flow of our cash and not by the cache of our cash.

But soon, we realize that the life we've built is controlling *us*— we're not controlling *it*. So we begin to focus on a fourth philosophy of wealth: one that prioritizes time. We assert ourselves as "Managers," taking control of our schedules and ensuring that we're squeezing every last ounce of value out of the lives that we lead.

Until one day we realize that we've squeezed all the value out of life and given nothing back. We begin to ask *why*. Why did we earn all of this money? Why did we save all of this money? Why did we acquire all of these assets? Why did we create all of this time?

Once we begin to ask these questions, we find that our philosophy of wealth turns inside out. No longer do we look to enrich ourselves—now we look to enrich those around us.

We begin to give back.

We begin making impacts.

And the more that we give, the more that we get.

We discover that the fastest path to wealth is the one that we chart through charity. We discover that helping others inspires others to help us. We discover that we didn't have to suffer through the false hopes of the Dreamer stage, the anxieties of the Settler stage, the volatilities of the Risk Taker stage, the existential crises of the Manager phase. We could have achieved wealth so much faster if we had pursued impact from the start.

We could have begun with the end in mind.

We could have begun as givers.

We could have begun with the intention of transforming the world.

I've found that the notion of transforming the world often intimidates people—it puts people off. They think that it simply sounds too outlandish—too *mythic* to be real. But here's the thing: You don't have to transform the world to *Transform the World*.

Just do what you can to help out your parents.

Do what you can to help out your kids.

Give to a cause that you believe in.

Share your philosophy with your family, your friends, your teammates.

You might not see how you've changed the world within a day or within a year. You might not even see how you've changed the world within your lifetime. But you *will* change the world.

Remember back to the previous chapter, when Dr. J. B. Jones gave a speech that inspired Earl Schoaff to give a speech that inspired Jim Rohn to give a speech that inspired Tony Robbins to feed a billion people.

That's the power of the Ripple Effect: you don't have to have Bill Gatesian, Warren Buffettian money to transform the world. You can do it with a single conversation.

It might just take a little while for the ripples to spread.

To many of us, achieving wealth and creating impact seem like impossible challenges. It's like we've been tasked with pushing a giant, granite boulder forward a mile. And it feels like the boulder isn't even stuck—it's actually rolling *backward*. It's *crushing* us. The debt is crushing us. The demands on our time are crushing us. The expenses, and the taxes, and the bills, and the rent. It's all just *pulverizing* us.

In that situation, you can't go from zero to sixty. You can't suddenly get control of the boulder and roll it wherever you please as fast as you please. You've got to work incrementally. You've got to find the right position for your hands. You've got to bend your elbows and plant your feet. You've got to resist, and then you've got to push.

And bit by little bit, you move the boulder forward.

Until, eventually, it stops being bit by little bit.

It starts to move a few feet at a time.

And then it starts to move yards at a time.

You gain momentum and you're in control and then, all of a sudden, you're not. All of the sudden, you find that you've built so much momentum that you can't stop the boulder. It's rolling—with or without you. And you're already a hundred yards past the mile marker.

Those are the physics of personal development. Those are the physics of financial growth and impact. It's hard at first, but it gets a little easier and a little easier and a lot easier and one day you wake up to realize that you're accumulating wealth faster than you can spend it—faster than you share it.

I've seen this happen firsthand. And not just once. I've seen it happen to clients over and over and over again. At the beginning of the process, people think that they will never ever be able to move the boulder—never, ever get out of the financial slump that they're in. And then one day, they find themselves calling me and saying that the earning is out of control. *Where do I put all this money?* they ask. *How can I protect it and steward it?*

And it doesn't necessarily take very long to gain that momentum either. A lot of people think that if you don't start in your twenties, you'll miss your shot, but that's just not the case.

I once met with a lady who was so old and fragile that she couldn't even drive herself to meet me. I've always been extraordinarily optimistic about what my clients can accomplish, but after spending a day with "Olive" and talking to her about what it would take to achieve wealth, I left thinking that she'd never be able to do it—that the meeting had been a total waste of time.

And I turned out to be wrong.

Very, very wrong.

Olive began working six days a week, seven days a week, *eight* days a week as the Beatles would have it. Within twelve months, her debt was gone, and she had a million dollars in the bank. Cross my heart and hope to die.

Wealth—*true* wealth, *impactful* wealth—can be achieved by anyone. By everyone.

Recognizing that is crucial to success. But it's also more than a little bit dangerous.

Not often, but every now and then, someone will hear my spiel and tell me that they're already at Stage Four, or they're already at Stage Five. As if to say that there's no work left to do. Anyone can achieve this, and they have, they say. They've already checked all the boxes that there are to check.

You might recognize this as a variation on the *Leave Me* mentality. "I've got it under control," this person says. "Trust me. I'm the biggest Humanitarian you've ever seen."

This attitude need not be—strictly speaking—*false*. It may very well be that this person *is* earning lots of money and *is* giving lots away. But if they think that means they're finished growing, then they're making a huge mistake.

You see, Humanitarianism relies on the cultivation and maintenance of an abundance mindset. But the abundance mindset isn't natural. To maintain an abundance mindset, we must constantly work to suppress our ingrained *scarcity* mindset. And that scarcity mindset can strike back at any time.

Unlike the abundance mindset, the scarcity mindset is hardcoded into our DNA. It's the product of millions of years of evolution—millions of years of hunting and gathering and keeping our enemies at bay.

We are not designed to *give*. We're designed to *survive*.

As a consequence, we can never truly rid ourselves of the scarcity mindset. No matter how much we achieve, we are always at risk of slipping back into Stage-One or Stage-Two thinking.

No matter how much we earn and no matter how much we accumulate, we find ourselves thinking, *If only I could make a little bit more this year.*

No matter how much we achieve and no matter how much we create, we find ourselves thinking, *If only I could stop working and play golf for the rest of my life.*

To achieve an abundance mindset and adopt a Humanitarian philosophy is an extraordinary thing. But it's not enough. Because wealth is not something that you *acquire*. It's something that you *practice*. Every minute of every day of your entire life.

Will LeBron James ever be good enough to stop practicing? Will Yo-Yo Ma ever be good enough to stop practicing?

Wealth can be made familiar.

It can be made comfortable.

It can be made accessible.

But it can never be *mastered*.

So we practice.

Part of practicing is teaching others. It's bringing people with you on your journey. In part because doing so will help you gain a better understanding of wealth's fundamental nature. And in part because doing so will give you a support system.

There *will* be days when you relapse—when you struggle to remember how you ever managed to achieve an abundance mindset—when the world looks scary and resources look scarce. And on those days, you will be grateful to have friends by your side who share your goals, share your vision, and refuse to let you be anything short of extraordinary.

Remember: We surround ourselves with people who are hungry, humble, and smart because they keep *us* hungry, humble, and smart.

In addition to teaching, the other essential strategy for keeping the practice of wealth alive is to never stop learning. Never stop attending lectures and workshops. Never stop asking brilliant people out for coffee. Never stop watching. Never stop listening. Never stop reading.

I also find it helpful to never stop *writing*. Really, I can't recommend writing enough.

Writing this book has been an incredible exercise in keeping my own Humanitarian practice alive. And now that I've written one book, I'm realizing that I want to write more. Lots more.

In the meantime, I've made a commitment to start blogging as often as I can. I've just bought a new domain name, and I've made a pact with myself that by the time this book is published, that site will be live with exercises and articles and wealth information of all kinds.

I hope that you'll join me there—at UnleashTheStages.com—so that wherever you are, and wherever I am, we can build a community of dreamers and givers together.

I know that I, for one, am going to keep inventing new exercises, keep building my support network, keep looking for new ways to send ripples out into the world. Because no matter how long I've been doing this, I will never become a master.

For each and every one of us, the pursuit of wealth is a lifelong practice—a lifelong journey.

We never become masters.

We never reach the end.

For each and every one of us, every day of the journey is the *first* day of the journey.

For each and every one of us, this is just the beginning.

Thank you, and I wish each and every one of you the best on your journey.

ABOUT THE AUTHOR

ERIC J. MORIN is the CEO and cofounder of Tower Leadership. He is a business and leadership consultant, as well as a Forbes speaker and author, who specializes in helping CEOs transform their businesses—and their lives—with a unique approach to wealth generation.

Eric's background includes building his own practice into a multimillion-dollar enterprise from the ground up. In the decades since, he has worked with thousands of business owners and individuals to help them spend less time in the office and more time doing the things they love.

Aside from private consultancy, Eric regularly speaks at events across the country. He has developed programs to suit almost any agenda—from keynotes and presentations to two-day workshops. In these keynotes, presentations, and workshops he has shown thousands of individuals how they can accomplish the same thing he has done by investing within the walls of their business or investing in their own personal development, turning their business or occupation from a simple income stream into a self-managed, wealth-generating asset that allows them to live the lives they have always wanted.

Eric's vision is to help as many business owners and individuals as possible achieve their vision and leave a legacy that they can be proud of.

To book Eric for your upcoming conference, visit EricJMorin.com. And to learn more about what Tower Leadership can contribute to your organization, visit TowerLeadership.com.

OUR SERVICES

TOWER LEADERSHIP is a unique organization that teaches business, leadership, and wealth skills to business owners. The goal is to reshape their lives to match their ambitions, carving out a work-life balance that enables business owners to positively impact their families, teams, and communities.

Tower Leadership helps impact companies through growth, processes, and culture. On the personal side, we show how to create wealth while reducing debt to put you on a path to leaving a legacy you can truly be proud of.